Praise for
The Emotionally Int
Teacher

'The Emotionally Intelligent Teacher *is a riveting read. Niomi explores the range of situations in which emotional intelligence comes into play. Her insights and analysis are extended through references to wider research. She has collated some heart-rending accounts of where relationships are undermined, and in some cases broken, by poor practices. These accounts are balanced by examples of professionals working well and humanely together. These colleagues pay as much attention to the "soft" stuff of emotions as they do to the "hard" metrics of running a school. A very helpful addition to the literature on school culture.'*

Mary Myatt, education writer,
speaker and curator of Myatt & Co

Niomi speaks with passion and purpose about the power of emotional intelligence, and how important it is in education to deal in a compassionate and supportive way with all those with whom we come into contact. She looks at how leading others in an emotionally intelligent way can support them to be their best. Niomi asserts that human connection, empathy, kindness and self-awareness are key. She raises the issues of whether emotional intelligence can be effectively measured and whether/how it can be developed and strengthened over time. Informed by her wider reading, she questions whether we can be successful in teaching and leadership if we lack it. Niomi draws on her own experiences and encourages the reader to revisit and reflect on their own. She cites a number of different educators who share their insights on the subject, and she uses case studies to consider emotional intelligence in specific contexts. This is an honest and courageous treatment of an important facet of human interaction.'

Dr Jill Berry, education writer, consultant
and former headteacher

The Emotionally Intelligent Teacher

Niomi Clyde Roberts

BLOOMSBURY EDUCATION

LONDON OXFORD NEW YORK NEW DELHI SYDNEY

BLOOMSBURY EDUCATION
Bloomsbury Publishing Plc
50 Bedford Square, London, WC1B 3DP, UK
29 Earlsfort Terrace, Dublin 2, Ireland

BLOOMSBURY, BLOOMSBURY EDUCATION and the Diana logo are trademarks
of Bloomsbury Publishing Plc

First published in Great Britain, 2022 by Bloomsbury Publishing Plc

This edition published in Great Britain, 2022 by Bloomsbury Publishing Plc

A catalogue record for this book is available from the British Library

ISBN: PB: 978-1-4729-7465-5; ePDF: 978-1-4729-7466-2; ePub: 978-1-4729-7467-9

2 4 6 8 10 9 7 5 3 1

Typeset by Newgen KnowledgeWorks Pvt. Ltd., Chennai, India
Printed and bound in the UK by CPI Group (UK) Ltd., Croydon, CR0 4YY

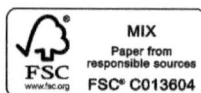

MIX
Paper from
responsible sources
FSC
www.fsc.org   FSC® C013604

To find out more about our authors and books visit www.bloomsbury.com
and sign up for our newsletters

I would like to dedicate this book to my much loved and dearly missed grandad, Desmond Connolly. He encouraged me to send my book proposal off to Bloomsbury and was one of the wisest and calmest people I have ever had the privilege to know. His Welsh roots meant that he was as determined and gutsy as he was calm. He relentlessly supported me and for this I am eternally grateful.

Contents

Acknowledgements

I would like to take this opportunity to thank the following educators who have contributed such insightful, fascinating and relevant case studies, opinions and experiences for inclusion in this book. These educators also contributed by summarising what they thought makes an effective teacher and leader – the results of this survey are collated later on in the book.

I feel that the book is far richer as a result of their contributions, and I will forever be grateful for their open, honest and transparent way of working with me.

Their wise words have inspired me, and hopefully they will strike a chord in your own experience and practice too.

Omar Akbar	Vic Goddard	Ritesh Patel
Ian Armstrong	Ronnie Hackett	Drew Povey
Jill Berry	Gavin Hosford	Stuart Rowntree
Andy Buck	Rebecca Keitch	David Shakeshaft
Heidi Collier-Brown	Johnathan Lear	Sam Strickland
Flora Cooper	Anoara Mughal	Stuart Wainwright
Andrew Cowley	Sarah Mulin	Matthew Watson
Mark Duffy	Mary Myatt	Scott Wellington
Nadine Finlay	Adam Newman	Paul Wright

A huge and heartfelt thank you to all.

Foreword

The turn of the century saw the emergence of the concept of emotional intelligence (sometimes referred to as 'EQ' or 'emotional quotient'). Setting aside the debate about whether this is an intelligence at all, or simply a set of personal competences, in his seminal article in 2000 for the *Harvard Business Review*, Daniel Goleman's model brought the idea to international prominence. He suggests that an individual's EQ is likely to be a much more important indicator of their effectiveness than their intelligence quotient (IQ). Of course, IQ is important, but Goleman argues that the thing that distinguishes standout performance is much more likely to be EQ. This makes a lot of sense to me. In schools, we need to deliver through others if we are to deliver great outcomes for pupils. We can't do everything ourselves, so building great relationships is critical.

In this book, Niomi Clyde Roberts has skillfully taken the key theory and research into this important area and brought it alive for both support staff and teachers, as well as for leaders working in schools. Full of case studies and practical examples, the book examines how self-awareness, self-management and the ability to recognise the emotions in others enable us all to build stronger relationships.

As Maya Angelou reminds us, 'people will forget what you said, people will forget what you did, but people will never forget how you made them feel'.

Andy Buck
Founder of Leadership Matters
Creator of the BASIC Coaching Method

Introduction

If you think that emotional intelligence doesn't belong in teaching and leadership, then you need to re-evaluate what underpins these roles. Emotional intelligence should run through every little vein – I'd even go as far as capillary – making a colossal difference to the way we interact with our colleagues, parents, children and, perhaps most importantly, ourselves. It should be the life-blood of everything we do because emotional intelligence is at the epicentre of every single interaction.

Throughout this book I will be commenting upon what emotional intelligence sounds like, what it looks like, what it feels like and how we can be better at delivering emotionally intelligent conversations. Other educators have provided insightful case studies about their experiences, which will help generate a complete understanding of why emotional intelligence is paramount.

The smallest comment

We, as teachers and leaders, need to be aware of how the smallest comment, action and even email can generate a wildfire of rage, and flames can spread quickly when greeted with an equally hot and turbulent response.

As educators, we know that having the emotional intelligence to understand and unpick emotional reactions – seeing beyond the behaviour – is so important when dealing with students and it is something that can have a significant impact upon how difficult scenarios play out. With our students, we aim to be nurturing, calm and consistent. We expect the same *from* our colleagues, but we should be *giving* it to them too.

As a teacher and leader myself, I have written this book because I believe sharing experiences while developing understanding heightens awareness. I am extremely passionate about emotional intelligence because I have seen first-hand examples of emotional intelligence in abundance, and I have also witnessed a severe lack of it. I have witnessed teachers and leaders that have used their emotional intelligence to handle difficult situations and the outcome has been positive and beneficial. I have also observed the flip side of this and encountered individuals with zero emotional intelligence, who cause absolute havoc, because they haven't reflected upon how their action or words may be received.

I want to help teachers and leaders who have found themselves in situations where they have felt at worst intimidated, patronised and victimised, and at best not listened to, quietened when they have a great idea and as though they don't belong. It is really important that teachers (especially newer teachers) realise that the problem is not necessarily with them; it may be, most unfortunately, the people around them. I want to help them see through the seemingly vindictive behaviour. Having a good sense of emotional intelligence allows you to forgive and move on, even if someone has purposely upset you.

With teachers and leaders in mind, I will be analysing, comparing and discussing the way we treat ourselves and our colleagues, with the idea of emotional intelligence at the very forefront. This book will also examine how we can lead people effectively and compassionately, ensuring that colleagues remain motivated and that high expectations are still very much achieved and sustained.

How can we, as educators, utilise our emotional intelligence to see beyond the situation and see the person in front of us?

How do we distance ourselves from the inherent power struggles, while continuing to be successful in our teaching and leading?

The answer to both of these questions lies in understanding ourselves and other professionals as humans, and being able to see and understand different perspectives alongside figuring out the *root* of the problem. These awareness skills make for the best possible teachers and leaders because understanding the 'how' and the 'why' of our own and others' emotions, while being able to positively navigate our way through them, is worth its weight in gold.

Detail matters. Understanding matters. Reaction matters.

1
Emotional intelligence and its place in education

Within our schools, daily workload, conversations and decisions seem to be run at quite some pace, and therefore the basics – thinking before speaking – can be quickly marginalised. A throwaway glance, or lack of a comment, can conjure up all sorts of anxious, defensive and impulsive reactions from colleagues. A single (perceived) negative experience can often put an educator on edge for the remainder of their working day.

Tone, words, reactions and sometimes silence are all indicators of how someone may be feeling. Just as with the students we teach, it pays to look closely at our colleagues' behaviour. Of course, there will be times when we are wrong and misinterpret a reaction, but more often than not, we can spot how someone feels just by watching their actions. I do honestly believe that actions supersede our words.

In many schools, the power struggles and politics can be silent, and not at all obvious to the outsider, unless you look very closely. Sometimes it is possible to achieve an understanding of how a school is run simply by walking inside and observing the day-to-day interactions. However, in order to identify the true culture of a school, you have to understand the principles and ethos underpinning this culture, while simultaneously studying the 'inside' energy and demeanour of all of the staff.

Within a school setting, a lack of emotional intelligence from the leadership can destroy the confidence, trust and sense of self of staff. Micromanaging to the nth degree doesn't benefit anybody. Trust, authenticity and freedom to explore new ideas is where the magic happens!

Being emotionally intelligent should naturally filter through everything we do within our school environments. It should be a substantial part of making decisions, having a meaningful conversation with a colleague and knowing when to intervene at the correct time, no matter what the circumstance is. Unfortunately, this isn't always the case, which is why I want to share examples, perspectives, unique 'inside' viewpoints and best practice. I want other educators to learn about how to navigate their teaching and leadership journeys, using human connection, intuition and a self-awareness that allows you to counteract the most negative of situations.

Before I continue, I really should outline what emotional intelligence means to me, in terms of the teaching world. This is very much open to interpretation, but here is my take:

Emotional intelligence is being fluent in understanding what makes you tick and how you deal with your own and others' emotions in the workplace. It is having a degree of sensitivity that allows you to question the wording of an email, reflect upon the quick note you leave for a teacher (who is extremely busy in their classroom) and handle those unnecessary comments that are made when you are exhausted. It is having the space to listen and respond to your emotions, while remaining calm under pressure.

Dr Jill Berry, author of *Making the Leap* (2016), thinks of emotional intelligence as 'the capacity to be aware of, control, and express one's emotions, and to handle interpersonal relationships judiciously and empathetically'. If we unpick the word 'capacity' we can already begin to think about whether some people naturally have this capacity to be aware of how someone else may feel or whether it is something that is learned (more on this on page 12). For some, understanding others and being empathetic may be alien.

Resistance to emotional intelligence

When somebody doesn't *have* the capacity to understand and doesn't *want* to develop their awareness, that's when obstacles are formed.

Some of us have a strong sense of emotional intelligence, as we have been through life experiences that have enabled us to develop and hone our understanding of empathy and understanding – what it may be like to walk in someone else's shoes. There are others that think inwardly and, for a multitude of reasons, cannot see beyond their own experiences.

I genuinely don't know the answer to teaching another person how to understand someone else's emotions; perhaps it cannot be done, but when a person is open to change and listens, I believe their understanding can develop somewhat. A small amount of emotional intelligence is better than none at all, right?

Over the last ten years I have honed my understanding of emotional intelligence and I've also had plenty of opportunities to put it into practice with colleagues, parents and my students.

I've always been very 'emotionally aware' and I'm pretty certain this is because I had to encounter many different and unwanted emotions as I was growing up. I have always been extremely aware of how others might feel and have always considered this in my daily communications and the consistency in my approach. I also work upon the basis of trying to take into account what is going on in someone's personal life. There is, more often than not, a reason for an individual acting the way they do; it's up to us as teachers and leaders to break down the barriers and delve that bit deeper, in a non-intrusive manner of course.

I've had plenty of experiences where I have had to delve that bit deeper, and examine the miscommunication, the anger, the wording and the error and think to myself, 'Why has this occurred? What may be the underlying problem?' Once I have considered these questions, I am then able to decipher my response in a sensitive but direct fashion.

Unfortunately, there are individuals out there that are unable to self-reflect or acknowledge their own emotions, and so this is when the resistance occurs. In many of the cases I've witnessed, it doesn't seem to end well. This can range from not understanding the students' emotions, as well as those of colleagues and parents, to a host of problematic situations, when an individual is unable to exercise the skills of self-awareness and empathy.

What does emotional intelligence look like?

Mutual respect and honesty

Honesty is an integral part of emotional intelligence and it is something that is very hard to build within a school culture, especially if mutual respect and trust are not present. Professional honesty needs to be built and autonomy should go hand in hand with this. If staff are not given the opportunity to be honest, there may be a fundamental lack of mutual respect.

High on my agenda is mutual respect. I'm sure you will agree that it is fundamental to a positive and successful school culture. I have always worked on this basis, both with students and with colleagues. I think working as part of a team and having a positive influence on others is vital, especially within school. As we all know, there can be negative cultures, individuals and procedures that can bring people down.

I've observed many teachers and have appreciated honest and reflective feedback when they have observed me. However, I have had occasions (as I'm sure we all have) where I didn't feel able to take a risk or I felt as though I had to deliver a lesson in a specific way because there wasn't mutual respect or trust between me and my observer.

It is possible to be honest *and* kind. You firstly appreciate the positives and the learning curve that the practitioner is on but you also respect them by being honest about what to try next. This type of feedback allows for the teacher to move forward with a willingness to risk-take but also a sense of 'I need to try this to improve' and a want to be even better, ultimately improving the learning experience for the children.

It really does make a substantial difference if your early career teacher (ECT), newly qualified teacher (NQT) or recently qualified teacher (RQT) mentor has a strong sense of professional honesty and the emotional intelligence required to help guide their thinking.

Mark Duffy, secondary school maths teacher in Basingstoke

During my training year, I was fortunate to have an amazing mentor. She was kind and helped me develop as a teacher, but she was also very honest with me. On one occasion I had not loaded up my lesson before a difficult class arrived from break. From the start of the lesson, the behaviour in the lesson made it difficult for learning to take place. My mentor knew that I wanted to be the best teacher I could be and she used this as a huge lesson for me. She was honest with me, let me see that the difficulties within the lesson were of my doing, and this was particularly difficult for me to hear. However, she knew how hard I would take it and ensured that she helped me unpick it properly and learn from it.

The students in our classrooms also need this honesty from us, but they also need us to be emotionally aware enough to know that the time and manner in which we are honest with them about their mistakes matter. Only when we show mutual respect are we able to ensure that students can learn from their mistakes.

As Mark points out, honesty is very important and so is the time at which this honesty is delivered. Reading the signals and acknowledging when, where and how you feed back works best.

Words matter

My external mentor was a lady called Ronnie Hackett and, to be quite honest, she was the only person that kept me going during my training year. She was an ex-headteacher and was strong and witty with bundles of emotional intelligence and, most importantly, she understood me.

I will go into detail about my training year, as I feel it is important, and it has made me a more resilient person and teacher because of what I experienced. I am also certain that others will be going through similar experiences currently. These words may provide comfort and reassurance.

I carried out my teacher training (Graduate Training Programme route) in a Year 6 classroom and my internal tutor very much taught me to have a tough skin. By that I mean that she would take most opportunities to tell me what I was doing wrong. I used to put on a brave face at school and cry most evenings. At the time, I just assumed this was completely normal as I had nothing to compare my experience against. Of course she may not have realised how much this affected me, but if she was aware of how her words may make others feel, then she may have reflected more.

I then went on to carry out a term's placement at another school and taught a Year 1 class. The mentor I had here was also very unsupportive and negative. I was more than happy to receive feedback, to move forward, but the way in which it was done left a lot to be desired. I was seen as far too passionate and apparently put too much effort into my teaching. I'm not entirely sure there is anything wrong with that — I was still learning, after all.

After the continuation of negative experiences, alongside having a teaching timetable of 95 per cent, Graduate Training Programme (GTP) training days, Masters assignments and collating evidence for my folders, I was feeling particularly drained most of the time. It was Ronnie Hackett who could see how hard I was working and made a point of saying, 'You're doing a great job!' Ronnie was the difference between me sinking and swimming.

Of course, when you are new into the profession, you don't want to alert anyone to what is happening and (as I did) you have a very real fear that the mentor will fail you. I still remember working especially hard to take on feedback and ensure I was up to date with the Teachers' Standards evidence and doing the very best I could, yet at every opportunity my mentor would make a remark that would slash my confidence and make me doubt my teaching ability. I am certain this kind of behaviour from leaders and mentors still exists, and it's just not acceptable. We don't do this to our students, so why would you do this to fellow colleagues and trainees?

This, as you can imagine, left me feeling pretty devastated, especially when Ronnie had praised my teaching, strong rapport with the children and how reflective I was in the classroom. I was utterly confused.

This negative behaviour was tough to experience in my NQT days, but when I became a mentor in my third year of teaching, it helped me think about my role and how important it was to get it right. I remember exactly how I felt as an NQT and thought very carefully about my words and actions. I applied the emotional intelligence daily that my internal mentors so desperately lacked.

As professionals we should never treat another person in a derogatory fashion, no matter what we may be going though outside of the school gates. I have had numerous times where I have been upset, feeling low or dealing with family situations. The difference is I've never allowed these events to dictate my professional behaviour towards fellow colleagues. Again, this is about emotional intelligence, being able to compartmentalise. Leave it at the door.

Of course, I am aware there are times when some people cannot leave their upset at the door. A private conversation with leadership about how they feel is the way forward in these situations, rather than acting out and upsetting others within the building. Again, it's about dealing with our emotions in a productive and calm fashion.

Intuition

You could refer to intuition as social sensitivity, as Daniel Goleman does in his book *Focus: The Hidden Driver of Excellence* (2013, pg. 113). Goleman suggests that social intuition 'tells us how accurate we are at decoding the stream of nonverbal messages people constantly send, silent modifiers of what they are saying'. So, in short, social sensitivity is about being able to read non-verbal clues. Reading non-verbal cues often includes trusting our gut instinct and having the experience and fine-tuned emotional intelligence to figure out exactly what is happening in a given situation.

In a school setting, teachers and leaders often have to make sense of the 'hidden' scenario with whatever limited information they have been offered; they have to use their intuition.

The questions I always ask myself when it comes to intuition are:

- Are some individuals naturally more emotionally aware than others?
- Do some individuals have an inbuilt social sensitivity to situations?

The answers to these questions depend entirely on the life experiences of the individual. They may have had to deal with difficult situations whereby their intuition and awareness were naturally developed, scenario by scenario.

After a helpful discussion about intuition on Twitter, Dr Jill Berry presented an interesting question that made me reflect upon my initial understanding of intuition. Jill posed the question: 'Is intuition just another way of stating "a good judgement"? Is there a specific difference?' I personally think that intuition can go hand in hand with judgement, as to form a judgement you need to have a strong understanding of the situation and potential consequences involved.

I think it is important to recognise here that not all teachers and leaders think that emotional intelligence and a strong sense of intuition are core elements that are needed in order to be a good teacher. Some educators believe that intuition doesn't belong within education, and therefore they fail to see how it may be relevant. Many believe intuition is 'wishy washy', with a 'mystical' element surrounding its meaning.

While many think this, I strongly believe that intuition, that very primal gut instinct, is at the very core of emotional intelligence. For me, it's the little signal that states 'something is amiss'.

Empathy and compassion

Empathy is essentially being able to place yourself in someone else's shoes and understand part of what they may be going through. I say 'part' because I don't think we have the true ability to understand 'completely' what someone is going through, as suffering is felt in many different ways. Compassion is being able to study someone's emotions and take action based on how they are feeling. It is being able to ascertain that there may be a valid reason for them to be acting in a certain way.

So, how often do we see empathy and compassion in our school environments? I'd like to think it would be present in the majority of school cultures, but I know that this isn't the reality. Unfortunately, it is one of the many reasons teachers have to move to other schools or leave the profession altogether. Nobody should be made to feel unvalued by another person. The way you treat someone else stays with that person, forever.

The idea of compassion as 'basic kindness' should ideally go hand in hand with a school culture. However, I'm sure we are all aware that this doesn't ring true in many schools. The concept of steadfast accountability has overridden much of the compassion and empathy that, for me, should form an integral part of a school's culture. Accountability needs to be present, but the way in which this is delivered person to person is where mutual trust, compassion and empathy need to be present.

Understanding someone as both a person and a professional is fundamentally important. You can still achieve high standards and you can still achieve good results while being empathetic and compassionate, working within the constructs and context of each individual.

Transparency

Transparency is another area that I've considered to be vital to emotional intelligence since stepping into the role of assistant head. I always used to question why leaders were never completely transparent and open about information. As someone who rates emotional intelligence and self-awareness very highly on my list of 'what makes a strong leader', I perhaps was naive to the fact that some information does need to be held back in certain situations in order to protect colleagues and ensure that issues are dealt with as efficiently and compassionately as possible.

Examples of having to keep some information back might include when you know that a colleague is having a tough time or going through a personal situation. Or maybe choosing not to tell a colleague that a parent has made a complaint about an element of their teaching practice, because actually it isn't the right time to. Or when a colleague approaches you to complain that their learning support assistant or higher level teaching assistant seems distracted, and you happen to know that this particular person is going through a difficult time in their personal life. It's not your place to divulge further detail; instead, it is to listen, observe and choose the correct time to sensitively take action.

It is always pertinent to choose the right time and place to reveal sensitive information to ensure that all parties are supported and feel appreciated as far as is possible. Before ploughing onwards and disseminating sensitive information, I always ask myself, 'Can this person take this information on at the moment? Would it be better to hold out until they are ready and focused?' Having said this, if I questioned every task in this fashion, nothing would ever be achieved! I am talking more specifically about sensitive matters here, rather than specific day-to-day curriculum tasks.

In my day-to-day processing, working alongside colleagues and dealing with sometimes emotionally charged situations, I try to stay as transparent as I can and I am always open to feedback. I want to ensure that decisions are reached correctly and fairly. I am now unbelievably aware of protecting staff from information that could lower their confidence or make them doubt themselves. In my position (alongside my headteacher), it is my job to encourage, protect and nurture – as well as keep uneasy feelings at bay, as much as realistically possible. This is not to say that I protect staff from everything, as sometimes people need a wake-up call and a 'teaspoon of reality' stirred gently into their thinking to help them improve their teaching practice or to reframe their thinking.

It is all about the right moment, the right tone and the right circumstances. We don't always get it right but as long as we openly admit our errors, take responsibility for our actions, reflect and improve, then we are making a key difference. We are also being as transparent as we possibly can – being genuine.

As a leader, sometimes you do your utmost to protect and nurture staff, but effort isn't always recognised, and this can be hard to adjust to. It's the subtle gestures, such as attending a meeting with them that they have requested for moral support, that sometimes aren't noticed or appreciated. But as a leader, that's something you have to just take in your stride. It's important to keep protecting and nurturing and actually, as long as you are aware it is happening and you see the benefits, does it need to be recognised?

Having open conversations and an open-door policy are important because it means that others are comfortable in voicing how they feel. Of course, it is always good to express how you feel in a professional way in a school environment. Not much good comes of flouncing around and making our emotions known throughout each corridor of the school; all this achieves is a negative domino effect and nothing gets resolved quickly.

Having an awareness of how you act under pressure, and how others may help and support you when this happens, is important. Awareness, reflection and ultimately change – that's when you know that someone is working hard to improve their sense of awareness. Awareness is a key player in the emotional intelligence stakes.

Awareness

I've observed leaders that do not have a single ounce of emotional intelligence and no desire to gain any awareness either. I don't have a problem with their lack of desire for self-improvement. My problem is this: it is how their behaviour makes other people feel.

There is a distinct difference between a teacher going home at the end of an exhausting day with negative thoughts of, 'I just can't do this anymore, I don't feel valued', compared with the positive thoughts of, 'Yes, I am exhausted but I am doing a good job – my efforts are being recognised'. It is all down to whether the leader chooses to recognise and value that teacher's effort. *It's how that person is made to feel.*

Far too often I have witnessed scenarios where a member of staff has walked away from a conversation in tears. Upon witnessing these situations, I've always said to myself, 'This is not how this situation should have been handled! Why on earth would you make someone else feel that way?' Granted, you cannot always hold yourself responsible for how someone else responds to a comment or gesture. However, if these comments or gestures were delivered in a kinder, more considerate way, perhaps the emotional reaction could have been avoided or lessened in some way?

My awareness of how others respond emotionally has increased significantly in the last couple of years. Feedback that I've taken on board has guided me, but for me it has been observing how others respond that has culminated in a better understanding. I always ask myself how I would feel in a given situation, and if I know it would make me feel uneasy, that tells me that it has been handled incorrectly. A prime example of this is if someone wandered into a classroom and, while a teacher was teaching, pointed out what they perceived to be negative points about their displays, before walking out – with nothing positive to say. That teacher is left feeling worthless when they are most likely to be already exhausted. How is that building them up? It's beating them with a stick when they are at their lowest. Newsflash – tearing people down in this manner does not work!

I think it is important to say at this point that I don't think anyone can be expected to fully understand another person. We can only ever understand a small fraction of that person, because our understanding is based on our senses – what we see and what we hear. We cannot view their innermost emotions. This is near-on impossible.

The complexity is this: sometimes what we see and what we hear are entirely different to what is actually felt.

Over time you can start to understand a person, but we humans are complex and, my goodness, as teachers we are very good at putting on a brave face! We often get on with the show, even when we are dealing with a multitude of unvoiced emotions behind the scenes.

Stuart Wainwright, former headteacher, English lead and now Standards and Excellence Officer for Suffolk

The key to emotional intelligence when motivating staff is to always be approachable and to always 'check in' with your staff every day. I would always walk round before the children arrived, say good morning and show a genuine interest in staff's wellbeing. If I knew they were doing something out of school the previous evening or at the weekend, I would ask about it with interest.

Another vitally important component of emotional intelligence is realising the challenges of the teaching profession; I would never ask of any staff what I wasn't willing to do myself and I would prioritise taking away any unnecessary tasks and paperwork that had no impact on themselves as teachers and the progress and wellbeing of the children.

Emotional intelligence and genuine empathy are the most vital ingredients for team spirit and a highly successful school!'

I had the pleasure of working with Stuart Wainwright in the early days of my teaching career. Stuart's positivity and understanding of his staff helped me thrive in my NQT year. This is one of the reasons why I am so passionate about how people are treated within school. When Stuart turned up at my school as deputy head towards the middle of my NQT year, he injected passion, empathy and a sense of purpose into each room he entered and he reinstated my fractured confidence. For this, I am truly grateful.

Self-reflection

As a new teacher, it can take time to understand why reaction and response can be fundamentally important to ensuring that interactions are both productive and, in many cases, positive. As you delve into the emotional reality of human nature alongside the daily marathon of the teaching world, it becomes apparent that to survive and flourish, self-reflection is 'up there' with knowing how to manage your time effectively.

Human nature indicatively means that at times we can be selfish. Many people are not taught how to self-reflect and so, if they don't naturally have this skill, it can be very difficult to develop. We see many examples of this in our day-to-day lives. I don't think I have to say too much around poor examples of self-reflection, as I think the last two years and how certain 'Covid' situations have been handled give you enough of an idea as to what I may be suggesting.

If you don't reflect upon why a situation didn't pan out as you had expected it to, then it is very likely that that type of situation will occur again. You can control the controllable but, granted, sometimes human nature and a busy school day can border upon the uncontrollable. And when this happens, it's good to acknowledge, reflect and say, 'I did my best'.

From a leadership perspective, we want to give our teachers the tools to manage their outlook and emotions effectively. However, sometimes this is easier said than done. While the developing of their own toolkit is in process, it is important to stay present and be there for when they need to talk through a situation. An example of 'just being there' for a colleague was when I was available to talk each morning before the school day. This helped this particular colleague to let off steam, so they would be ready to start the school day refreshed. They came into my classroom for a term or two as I was setting up each morning, and talked about what was worrying them. They were able to offload. This helped them get through their school day successfully and, as time passed, they eventually managed without.

This member of staff was self-reflective and understood that she needed time to offload before the school day and also a safe space where she felt comfortable to do this.

Effective leadership is providing that little stepping stone in between the 'realisation, reflecting and then eventually actioning themselves' stage – teaching them to coach themselves as effectively as possible, reflecting, adapting and responding in the best way they possibly can, and thus self-reflecting and positively adapting to the 'given' situation.

Nature or nurture?

Is emotional intelligence something we learn over time based on what we experience in our lives, or is it something innate that some people are genetically equipped with while others are not?

At a Cambridge Teaching event in 2018, I had a discussion with fellow teacher Matthew Watson about whether you can 'learn' to be emotionally intelligent. He said, 'I don't know if people can learn emotional intelligence just like they can't learn empathy. Maybe it's like sympathy – something you can't fake if you don't feel it.'

Matthew may have a point. Is it simply the case that some people have it in abundance and others just don't? It's a little like the old Maybelline advert slogan: 'Maybe they're born with it'. Or, in some cases, not!

Matthew and I also discussed how you could monitor and evaluate someone's sense of emotional intelligence, other than giving them situations where their reactions would be judged, much like a psychometric assessment. Even then it would be tricky to obtain a genuine picture. I'm sure you'd agree.

How do we study and evaluate emotional intelligence?

Can psychometric assessment easily identify those with high or low emotional intelligence, or do you think it is delivered, shown and demonstrated through actions? Reflect on your own thoughts before you read any further.

In answer to this line of enquiry, Drew Povey told me that, 'my strong belief in this area is two-fold. Firstly, I am a big fan of the Hay Group's psychometric to rate an individual's levels of emotional intelligence. I have used this with many people over the years to great success. However, a test like this is never perfect and should not be used in isolation. I also feel it is important to observe the behaviour of a person to see if this plays out in reality. Some simple questions to students, clients, staff and key players will give more colour to the canvas. When a mixture of a test, observation and questioning is implemented, a well-rounded view of emotional intelligence can be gained.'

This begs the following questions: Should we be ensuring that our leaders carry out a test that really does delve into their emotional understanding of people and situations? Can emotional intelligence truly be learned on the job? And can we be successful as a teacher and leader without this essential skill?

Mary Myatt suggests that to be an emotionally intelligent teacher and leader, you should have 'the ability to monitor your own and other people's emotions, to discriminate between different emotions and label them appropriately, and to use emotional information to guide thinking and behaviour'. I think the monitoring aspect is so important because if you are not 'checking in' with how you feel and responding accordingly, then emotions can spiral out of control quite rapidly.

Sam Strickland, author and principal of Duston School

A hugely important trait of being an emotionally intelligent leader is the ability to take your time. It is seductive to make fast, high-speed decisions and to portray an impression to others that you are busy. As a result, they should also be busy. I think this is a false economy. The very best and most effective leaders take their time over changes or decisions; they communicate the changes effectively to every layer of the school, thus ensuring that the understanding surrounding the change is firmly embedded before it goes live.

The best leaders are also emotionally rich. They understand that a teacher requesting to see their five-year-old in their first ever Christmas play is really important to their colleague. They understand that some staff need a well done, a pep talk, some TLC or maybe a boost.

Day to day, the best leaders practise what they preach, permit what they promote and promote what they permit.

They not only talk the talk but also walk the walk.

I completely agree with Sam here; the majority of people don't request time out unless it is important to them. Each situation is, of course, different; however, there is such a thing as flexible consistency. You still keep the standards high, but you adapt to each individual and each context – showing that you care.

I will finish this chapter with a case study about experiences of emotional intelligence. I met Nadine while studying on our GTP teaching course. Nadine is a fantastic teacher and now a leader. Here is her take on emotional intelligence within teaching.

Nadine, teacher and leader at a school in the West Country

Emotional intelligence is a skill that leaders need the most. Time to take a breath, think and reflect before they act. Since becoming a leader myself, I am striving to develop higher levels of emotional intelligence but I have not always had the best role models.

Throughout my career I have been fortunate enough to work for a variety of different principals and have used these experiences to shape how I am becoming a leader. When thinking about emotional intelligence, I have always understood that it has several different main traits: self-awareness, self-regulation, social skills, motivation and empathy.

I believe that to be a leader means that you need to have and to demonstrate each of these different characteristics to those you interact with each and every day. Sadly, this is not always the case.

Self-awareness and self-regulation

Self-awareness and self-regulation often go hand in hand as it's impossible to regulate your own behaviour if you are unaware of it. One headteacher I worked for openly struggled

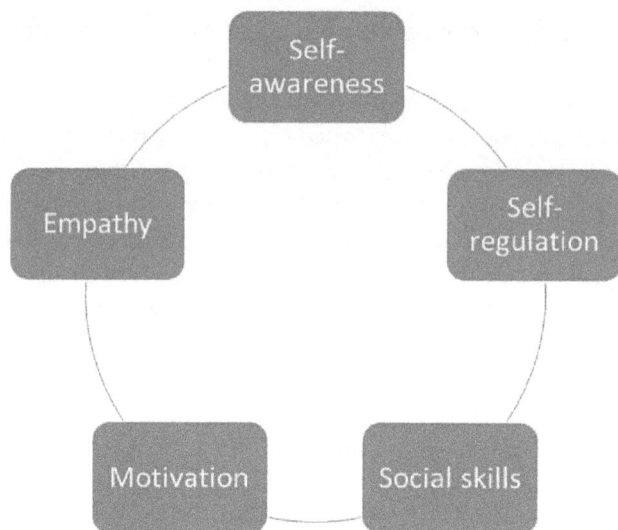

Figure 1: The main traits of emotional intelligence

with each of these traits. She had achieved headship in an unprecedented amount of time and hadn't had the opportunity to learn about each of the key stages in significant detail. She had mainly taught in Key Stage 1 prior to becoming a headteacher and this had meant that she was playing catch up with EYFS and Key Stage 2. Her personal uncertainty triggered moments of sporadic motivation, where she was desperately trying to experience particular things that were happening around the school, while at the same time running the school. Unfortunately, this inconsistency caused her excessive stress and she found that managing her stress levels was almost impossible.

An example of this was midway through Year 6 SATs. The Year 6 teacher had been speaking to her in the office and there had been frayed tempers on both sides. As my Year 6 colleague left the office, I knocked and stepped in, just as the headteacher picked up a handful of pens and threw them at the open office door, after the Year 6 teacher. As I had just walked in, they hit me and landed on the floor. Unfortunately, this was not a one-off occurrence; it became apparent that throwing pens at an open, empty doorframe was a stress management technique that the head used from time to time, much to the detriment of passers-by.

Social skills

In order to be a respected and effective leader, conquering and demonstrating key social skills is of vital importance. You will find yourself in situations where you need to form a relationship in quite a short period of time, and an effective strategy to achieve this is to make eye contact. To hold a conversation and not make eye contact with the recipient is something that many find challenging, as people react to others' facial movements. To make eye contact shows that you are focused and paying attention. I, of course, am aware that eye contact may be sensory overload for some individuals.

In one school I worked in, every Friday, as many schools do, we would invite parents in to the celebration assembly. It was during this time that I began to notice that the headteacher was unable to make eye contact with any of the parents. In fact, when thanking the families for coming in, she would look at the floor. Public speaking is a skill in itself, but as a leader it is vital that we generate a sense of reassurance and calmness. Parents are entrusting us with their most prized possession; the least we can do is look up and show mutual respect when we speak to them. We should consider that there could have been a genuine reason as to why she couldn't make eye contact. If this is the case for you, ask for support and help from others so that people are aware of 'why'.

Another school I worked in held a pupil progress meeting quite soon after I'd joined. There had been a high amount of staff mobility and one class was being taught by a long-term supply teacher, Mr A*. This supply teacher had decades' worth of teaching experience and had recently taken time out of class to travel. He was keen to be back in the classroom but had plans to travel again the following year, which is why he'd decided to be supply cover instead of permanent. His second week with the school happened to be the termly assessment week. After marking 29 papers for reading, maths, grammar, punctuation, spelling and arithmetic within this week – a great ask for any teacher, especially someone who is non-permanent – Mr A attended the scheduled pupil progress meeting. As a new member of the SLT, I had been invited to this particular meeting and was shocked to discover that Mr A was sitting in a lonely chair on one side of the board table, while on the other side sat the head, the deputy headteacher (who was assessment lead), the maths coordinator, the English coordinator and myself (the Read Write Inc. lead). We were each given time to question Mr A about how the children in the class were progressing in relation to our subject focus. Understandably, poor Mr A was feeling slightly unnerved by this and, to add another element, he was then asked to complete an old-style APP tracking grid for every child (the APP tracking grid is an enormous grid with statements for every single objective the child should be meeting) so that he could gain a deeper grasp of the children's level of understanding. Thankfully, Mr A stood up against this unbelievable request and refused. There was no way he was willing to carry out, mark and analyse 110+ test papers within a week, along with completing an APP assessment in reading, writing and maths. This lack of empathy highlighted to me just how out of touch the leadership team was with the rest of the staff. It has haunted me for years. Since this incident, I have always insisted that pupil progress meetings I'm involved in will be an open discussion about each individual child and where they currently are in their learning, so that there is never to be a repeat of this unfortunate incident.

Motivation

One headteacher I worked with had very specific techniques to motivate staff, which always focused around teacher wellbeing, of sorts. On the very first day of term, he would hire a canal boat and take the whole staff for a trip down the canal for group bonding – a huge success for all involved! On training days he often brought several health experts into school to take cholesterol levels, check the curvature of the staff's spines, provide head massages and teach yoga breathing. When I reflect on it now, I'm sure it was kindly meant but I'm not entirely convinced about how motivational it was for colleagues to be told that they had high cholesterol levels or they needed to head out and purchase an orthopaedic mattress before permanent damage was caused to their spine.

That being said, I have known leaders who, as a means of supporting their work–life balance, will intentionally give their staff time out of their classroom during their assessment week so they can get all of the marking done during the school day.

A dear friend of mine recently became a headteacher and has blocked out one afternoon each week to be able to get back into classrooms, cover for the teachers and give them an extra PPA slot each term. The benefit for her is that she now knows every child in the school by name and has a rapport with them all, while her staff feel supported with the ever-growing workload that teachers have.

I've also known heads who, when teams are staying late to refresh wall displays in corridors or rebuild the outside gardening area, have ordered takeaway pizza for the volunteers. These may be small token gestures but they've made such a difference to staff morale.

Empathy

To have empathy with staff and children is of vital importance. Yes, we all have ideal deadlines and routines that we try to stick to, yet when working with people it always needs to be recognised that our emotions, along with personal historical baggage, will affect this. One woman I was working with had struggled for a long time with fertility, and without realising she became very aggressive towards colleagues when they fell pregnant and started their own families. This behaviour was involuntary yet it had an effect upon the working environment.

On the other hand, I have worked for principals where they take the time to meet with staff regularly just to listen, to enable them to have the opportunity to chat about life outside of the school walls and develop trust. I've seen this trust blossom into a relationship where the staff felt supported and acknowledged, which in turn meant that they were happier in their workplace and would often go the extra mile.

Overall, it could be very easy for teachers to feel disheartened with leadership that is not emotionally intelligent. However, I have never met a leader who has intentionally set out to do a bad job or make someone's workplace utterly miserable. This isn't to say that those people aren't out there, but they are few and far between. Instead, there are leaders who are still working on developing emotional intelligence. No one is perfect.

As a teacher who's trained and worked in both the private and public sector, with children aged from Foundation Stage 1 all the way through primary school, I have had the good fortune to see the impact a teacher has on the children within a class. They are a positive role model in all they do; therefore, by extension, a leader who strives to be a positive role model, demonstrating confident emotional intelligence to their staff, will also have an unmistakeable effect upon their team. As leaders we must not forget this.

*Name changed for anonymity

Thought capsule

Just as you can notice the culture of a school pretty much as soon as you walk through the doors, you can also sense the amount of emotional intelligence a team of teachers and leaders have between them.

2
Empathy

Empathy is more of a force than intuition, compassion and honesty, which is why a whole chapter has been dedicated to it. Within this chapter there will be discussions around the different types of empathy and also antipathy – the opposite of empathy. While recognising the differing states of empathy/antipathy, there will also be examples of how it is seen and drawn upon when it is at play in our schools.

'Empathy underlies many facets of moral judgement and action.' (Goleman, 1995, pg. 105) But what if there is amoral judgement – how does empathy exist then? This poses a number of important questions:

- If an individual does not naturally have an inbuilt moral compass, how can they identify with others in an empathetic way?
- Is empathy learned?
- Are people born with differing amounts of empathy?

These are questions I genuinely don't know the answers to, and to be perfectly honest, I don't think anyone does. There is research into these questions, of course, but no definitive answers.

Different forms of empathy

Humility

I believe that having a modest, humble opinion of oneself goes hand in hand with being a reflective and empathetic teacher and leader.

'For leaders of all stripes, reconnecting with our values – with our truest, deepest instincts – is an essential building block of character, which is the essence of leadership. And it begins with humility.' (Kerr, 2013, pg. 17)

Being transparent and genuine does make such a difference; personally, I see straight through the 'talk' and look beyond, and I'm very quick to tell whether the person is being genuine and true. I think most people have a gut instinct that tells them what they need to know. I base 95 per cent of my decisions around my gut instinct. I leave around five per cent for a tiny little snapshot of logic – but I've never been let down (so far!).

I think humility is having that genuine care about the people around you and also the willingness to admit when you are wrong. Both children and adults see straight through the talk when someone isn't being genuine or showing a level of humility. A leader may say to a teacher, 'I'm here for you', but if those words don't match their actions and day-to-day behaviour, then that teacher won't trust the leader enough to open up to them. Words (in this case) need to go hand in hand with effort and actions – otherwise they hold very little value.

Stuart Rowntree, member of SLT and Year 6 teacher in Tees Valley

It is the 'understanding others' that makes my job so worthwhile. I think once you understand that emotion is the root to the majority of responses and that knee-jerk reactions are just the surface of what is going on beneath, it helps form an empathy that makes you ask, 'But why?'. It's a part of the journey that I revel in. It's challenging and it's really very frustrating at times, but developing a key understanding of another soul – be that an adult or a child – is a serious undertaking and should be met with a sense of personal growth and achievement.

As Stuart suggests, getting to know our colleagues well can be frustrating and onerous at times, but it is certainly a worthwhile venture.

Teachers and leaders who understand that they don't always have an answer are the most effective. They don't pretend to be 'The Big I Am'; they show their humility and dignity, and will admit when they are wrong or unsure.

Here are a few statements that demonstrate how leaders can use their language and opportunities to show that they are still human beings, and open to error – as all of us are. The power and use of words and terminology is critical in these examples:

'Thanks for correcting me. I didn't realise that.'
'I hadn't thought about it like that; I understand now.'
'I was wrong about that; your thoughts have made me change my mind.'
'I should/would like to do some more research before I give a viewpoint.'
'I'm more than happy to be proved wrong as I know I don't always get it right.'

Of course, in the heat of the moment, some leaders do get it wrong and this is when hot emotions hijack thinking and responding. Everyone makes mistakes from time to time, but it is so important to learn from them. Being aware of our trigger points means that we can respond in a calm, centred and reasonable manner. Anger, judgement and misunderstanding (as we well know) don't resolve anything.

Connections

Humans look for connections: they look for smiles; they look for glances; and they scan for body language when someone is talking. We are so perceptive to all of this and we take in all this information quickly. We absorb what we see. So in conversations, before a word has been uttered, you begin to get a sense of how a discussion might pan out.

At this point, let's refer to and reflect upon the decision cycle created by strategist John R. Boyd. Boyd states that 'to maintain an accurate or effective grasp of reality, one must undergo a continuous cycle of interaction with the environment to assess its constant changes' (Kerr, 2013, pg. 26).

'Observe
This is data collection through the senses; visual, auditory, tactile, olfactory, taste – as well as more modern metrics. Like an animal sniffing the wind, we gather the raw material for response.

Orient
This is analysis, synthesizing all available data into a single, coherent 'map of the territory' – a working theory of our options.

Decide
This is the point of choice, where we determine the best course of action. We cut away the extraneous by making a decision.

Act
We execute; acting swiftly and decisively to take advantage of the moment. We then go back to the beginning and observe the effect of our actions. And so the loop continues.' (Kerr, 2013, pg. 27)

This decision loop is very similar to the way in which we conduct conversations. As a teacher and leader, I think the 'observe' and 'act' stages are critical. If you are 'in the moment' and 'reading' the person who is in front of you, then stepping in when you need to or clarifying a thought at exactly the right moment will be indispensable.

The reason many of us feel so strongly about kind, considered conversation is because it boils down to the fact that you have absolutely no idea what is happening behind closed doors in someone's life. Teachers are incredible at putting on a 'front', even when inside they aren't feeling at their best. So, we are good at tricking others into thinking that we are fine and dandy, when in fact, the reality can be quite the opposite.

This is precisely why we should have more conversations, rather than emails. In a conversation, you can see the other person's body language, their tone, their facial expressions – none of which you can grasp from behind a computer screen. Sam Strickland (2020, pg. 77) states that 'the key to restricting email use is to ensure that staff have sufficient face-to-face directed time to meet and discuss items in person. It also helps when the senior team themselves agree core messages and send out only one or two messages a week, rather than hundreds of emails. Giving staff time is key.'

It's important to recognise that there are always going to be outside influences and these can get in the way of the heavy workload of school life. Being aware of your team's emotional wellbeing is high on the agenda. However, it is important not to let standards slip. If you need to be flexible, be flexible. For example, if it is taking a colleague slightly longer to complete a task, don't pile on the pressure by creating an unrealistic deadline just because you can; meet them halfway. Trust them; after all, they are professionals! Pick up on the silence. Read the words that are unsaid. Silence is a form of communication after all.

If an individual is unhappy, feeling the pressure or feeling that they are not listened to, their standard of work will automatically slip. Catch them, communicate and let them know you are available before this happens. Ideally, you would have developed a strong rapport prior to this point, so that this wouldn't occur.

I know you've all heard this phrase countless times before but, as Bananarama said, 'It ain't what you do, it's the way that you do it!' You've heard this so many times before because it's so fundamentally true. For those younger readers, this song lyric refers to acting in a certain way to achieve positive results.

How you feel determines whether you stay and do well in your job – or whether you leave because you didn't feel happy with the way you were treated. There must be trust, transparency and respect. There has to be an apology if you get things wrong, and there has to be challenge – but kind and respectful challenge. There is no room for ego, no room for spitefulness and certainly no room for manipulation. This is not true leadership and, if you ever come across this in your working life (which I'm sure you will), I would look for the opportunity to change workplace as soon as possible – you don't deserve to be treated that way. Nobody does. Some people (like myself) put up with it for years and then eventually come to the realisation that nothing will change. If you are anything like me – extremely determined and sometimes quite stubborn – you will work hard to try to overcome the challenges, but there comes a time when you realise you are not appreciated and that it is basic self-respect to move on and look after yourself.

I've witnessed so many conversations that have left colleagues feeling low. The problem is that words stay with us. A very relevant example of this was during my training year. My main mentor and my mentor at my second placement were having a conversation about me, and within earshot one said, 'She takes one massive step forward and then several steps backwards.' That was just her perception, but it was horrible to hear. Perhaps I'm sensitive, but it really did feel like I should just give up there and then! Luckily, I am too stubborn to quit like that, and despite the negativity and attempt to bring me down, I carried on. I fought back, but that doesn't mean it didn't really hurt me. I doubt myself because of comments like these, even to this day. These kinds of comments are unprofessional and have no place in any workplace, let alone a school.

Conversations between staff at school, at any level, should be kind and focused and should leave each person feeling valued and trusted – even when it is a 'difficult conversation'. The goal of a difficult conversation should be to resolve an issue – to give an honest account of what is happening and to find a way forward. I am not naive to the fact that sometimes these conversations can take an unpredictable turn, but I think the true leader should facilitate and instigate a positive way forward, considering the other person's feelings and reflections. Gavin Hosford, a headteacher in West Yorkshire, says, 'There are no difficult people; it's just our perception of them. There may be difficult conversations, but depersonalising the conversation like I try to do, and I know many others do, helps massively – I will start the conversation with something like, "In my role as headteacher, I need to talk to you about…" rather than starting the conversation with a personal thought or feeling.' This strategy removes the emotion from the conversation so that both parties can remain open and logical – because as we all know, our emotions can be irrational at times, especially when we feel strongly about a situation.

Leading with empathy

Kindness and empathy may be viewed as a weakness by other leaders or staff in your school. This just further highlights a lack of understanding of what emotional intelligence fundamentally is. It is not a weakness; if anything, it is a strength. Being empathetic does not mean you have lower standards; it means you are willing to be flexible to achieve high standards. I know this because I maintain high standards when working with my team, alongside being empathetic, and so I *know* it can be achieved. I've seen other leaders with similar outlooks achieve a great deal of success with their teams.

Listed below are some leadership traits that I consider to be crucial:

- clear communication
- drive
- empathy
- focus
- high expectations
- kindness
- motivation
- transparency.

If you remove 'kindness' and 'empathy' from this list of leadership attributes, you could be left with a leader who is cold and calculated. A leader that has a strong level of emotional intelligence but uses this as a power tool over others, almost in a predator-like fashion, targeting those who are seemingly vulnerable in the workplace. I'm sure many of us have witnessed the effects of this type of leadership first-hand. It is one of the many reasons I'm writing this book! It is also why I want to help other teachers and leaders avoid going through difficult and agonising scenarios as a result of someone else's actions.

In June 2020, I posed a question on Twitter: 'What makes an "emotionally intelligent teacher and leader"?' I received an extensive list of attributes from fellow teachers:

- adaptable
- allows autonomy
- authenticity
- compassion
- consistency
- courageous
- depth of knowledge
- empowers others
- fairness
- grows others
- honesty

- humility
- integrity
- listener
- loyalty
- no ego
- patience
- pragmatic
- realistic
- reflective
- respectful
- sense of humour
- someone who notices
- team over self
- trustworthy
- vulnerability.

I have found, and continue to find, other people's perspectives really valuable and agree with them whole-heartedly. Ultimately, a leader should be someone who shares the credit and shoulders the blame. It would be really tricky to suggest top attributes from this list, as all of them combined create the character behind a strong leader: quiet efficiency. No bold, pressuring or egotistical comments, just seamless, calm ticking-over, allowing everyone to work to the best of their ability.

Goleman's empathy triad

As mentioned at the beginning of this chapter, antipathy is the opposite of empathy. Perhaps this is quite a strong view but I can honestly say I have come across leaders that are completely unaware of how their actions may negatively affect people – and quite significantly too. If you have ever come across someone like that, you too have probably questioned whether or not they even have an empathy toolkit available to use. In some cases, this leader isn't just unaware of their actions, they have absolutely no idea that they are in the wrong; they are lacking *cognitive empathy*.

So what is cognitive empathy? And while we're discussing this, we may as well delve into 'emotional empathy' and 'empathetic concern', otherwise known as Goleman's 'empathy triad' (Goleman, 2013).

Cognitive empathy allows us to 'take other people's perspective, comprehend their mental state and at the same time manage our own emotions while we take stock of theirs'.

Emotional empathy is when 'we join the other person in feeling along with him or her; our bodies resonate in whatever key of joy or sorrow that person may be going through'.

Empathetic concern is when 'this compassionate attitude builds on bottom up primal systems for caring and attachment deep down in the brain' (Goleman, 2013, pg. 98).

With these different forms of empathy identified, it is important to note that a darker side of cognitive empathy emerges when someone uses it to spot weakness in others and so takes advantage of them. David Shakeshaft examines how this can sometimes be the case.

David Shakeshaft, headteacher in Birmingham

You should use emotional intelligence with care and humanity – I know a few leaders who have it in abundance but use it manipulatively. There is a 'Derren Brown' side to leadership (control and manipulation) that can be abused, a combination of good psychology and power trip leadership.

I had a tough conversation with a former colleague – she's a master at working out what makes people tick. I had plucked up courage to have an open conversation and felt on the back foot when she said, 'Well you've clearly rehearsed that – let's unpick it.' She knew that would throw me and it played on my propensity for self-doubt that led to a lack of confidence – something I had confided in her before I realised she was manipulative.

These are good points well made by David. Until I experienced it myself, I was completely unaware of how a person could use empathy in a manipulative fashion. Perhaps I was naive and far too trusting, as many of us are.

It is a shame that people would actually try to use their empathetic toolkit to their advantage, to 'pull the wool over someone's eyes'. It strikes me as having a motive, and that motive being to prey on someone else's vulnerability. The reason I think this 'side' of empathy, and how it can be used in school, is important to bring up is because undoubtedly many of us will experience this at some point during our teaching careers. It is better to be wise to it than to be left feeling manipulated.

Barriers to empathy

When people are mistreated, humiliated, patronised or conditioned to be something they are not, invisible barriers are naturally formed. Barriers are a person's way of protecting themselves against anxiety, hurt, high expectations, new ideas, etc. As a teacher or leader, you will need to break down many barriers to succeed in your role. This takes time and plenty of effort and it can be exhausting at times – but it really is worthwhile! Once you've managed to get that person or people 'on side', the interactions and working alongside them become so much more manageable and enjoyable. While helping break down those barriers, you also build that sincerity of trust, and once that is developed, it should be maintained and celebrated.

Change

No one likes change, but sometimes it's necessary. A natural human response to change is to say 'not today!', which is why leadership roles (or any roles) that encourage movement and change can be mentally exhausting.

In September 2018, I had the experience of joining an already formed team and had my work cut out for me as I had to break down many barriers. I joined as Year 5 leader and part of the senior leadership team. It took a few months, but eventually I was able to reach those members of staff that had originally not warmed to me, mainly because I was new and had different or higher expectations. This is where I learned that face-to-face interaction is so much more valuable than emails because you can judge the whole picture, see their body language, observe their facial expressions and hear the tone of their voice. My colleagues soon realised that my actions matched my words and that I had their backs if they needed to discuss anything with me. They also knew that I was there for the children, and that, for me, being part of SLT was not a power trip. I wanted to see, encourage and make change for the better. Status does not matter; the type of person you are and how you treat others does!

The bias towards negative emotions

John Tierney and Roy Baumeister (2020) define negative bias as 'the universal tendency for negative events and emotions to affect us more strongly than positive ones'. I think many of us within this profession are guilty of ignoring positive feedback when it is received alongside one negative comment. Guess which comment we ruminate over? The negative comment, of course! It's either human nature or teacher nature, one of the two. The root of this negative bias can often be rooted in a positive one – the need to improve. We can either let a negative comment floor us or we can take the comment, think about it, get cross about it, feel stubborn about it, but ultimately respond to the comment with a proactive attitude. Change a negative to a positive. Show that we are capable of coming back stronger, and that criticism (when delivered in the right way) can actually be very positive. It is all about perspective!

Time and time again, research has shown that cognition and feeling (emotions) are invariably linked. We know this to be true but for some people the ability to manage making decisions alongside emotional response is still somewhat varied. You have the emotionally intelligent teacher or leader who can process their emotions and seem calm on the outset, or you can have a teacher or leader who doesn't hide any of their emotions and very much makes their anger, frustration or upset known – normally rather loudly. Reference to this type of teacher or leader can be found in Chapter 1, where a teacher witnessed pencils being thrown at a door in a fit of rage.

Decision making and affect

Without emotions, our decision making would be uninformed. Emotions run through many gates, presenting us with instant information and vital clues about a situation. Of course, the effectiveness of these gates depends on the type of emotion being felt. When the logical compartment of a brain is blocked, of course there does tend to be an irrational and illogical response, which in turn has to be worked through.

I'm sure we all know a leader who makes steadfast decisions with little thought of their emotional output or of the wellbeing of others around them. This may be a conscious decision – 'I feel this way but I will ignore that feeling and plough on regardless'. However, it may be a completely subconscious approach, where over time this person has learned to ignore or bat back their emotional response, therefore inducing an almost numbing effect where the cognitive message continuously speaks ever louder than the emotional message. I still find it fascinating, and shocking, that when I have spoken to others outside of education about emotional intelligence, they have not heard of it and nor do they think it holds any importance to their interactions. This worries me considerably.

If we accept that without our emotions, our decision-making ability is impaired, then surely the decisions made by someone who isn't consciously accessing their emotional output are lacking judgement and are void of empathy and perspective? 'One of the ways by which emotions work is through neurochemicals that bathe particular brain centres and modify perception, decision making and behaviour. These neurochemicals change the parameters of thought.' (Norman, 2005) When a person makes a decision to ignore emotional output, it stunts the pathways within their brain and reduces their ability to use empathy to guide their thinking.

It's interesting to recognise that in some cases the affective system can work against the cognitive system, as detailed above. It's fascinating because your physiological response system seems to be in play constantly, especially when speaking in public. You could be one of the most confident people out there and still become nervous when speaking in front of others. Is this purely down to previous experiences or to how our brain responds to an overload of cognitive thought processes? For example, when standing in front of a room full of adults, whoever you are, I am pretty certain at least one of the following questions will pop into your head, among many other often irrational thoughts:

How will I come across?

Do I look OK?

Why am I suddenly sweating?

Are they going to judge me?

Am I talking too fast or too slow?

What if I stumble over my words?

What if their expressions show boredom?

How can I tell whether they are genuinely interested?

Norman (2005) suggests that 'the affective (emotions) and cognitive systems are thought to work independently, but they influence one another, with the former operating unconsciously while the latter operates at the conscious level'. Think about a time you were in the classroom and derailed by an unruly pupil, frozen in an interview or unexpectedly told off by a horrid senior leader on a power trip. How did you react?

Intuitive empathy

I've always been a firm believer in 'gut instinct', and I've found that when something 'feels' wrong or I have an uneasy 'feeling' then generally that feeling is spot on. This demonstrates that our gut instinct is a result of unconscious cognitive thought. 'Intuition or gut feelings are also the result of a lot of processing that happens in the brain. Research suggests that the brain is a large predictive machine, constantly comparing incoming sensory information and current experience against stored knowledge and memories of previous experiences, predicting what will come next.' (Van Mulukom, 2018)

As suggested in Chapter 1, some people may pass off the word 'intuition' as something that perhaps is a little 'fluffy' as it doesn't involve a logical thought process. However, what it does involve is a primal instinct, one that is already built into our nervous system. So surely it would be wise to take note of the warning signals it fires out? 'Intuition and gut feeling bespeak the capacity to sense messages from our internal store of emotional memory – our own reservoir of wisdom and judgment. This ability lays at the heart of self-awareness and self-awareness is the vital foundation skill for the three emotional competencies:

Emotional Awareness: The recognition of how our emotions affect our performance and the ability to use our values to guide decision making.

Accurate Self-Assessment: A candid sense of our personal strengths and limits, a clear vision of where we need to improve, and the ability to learn from experience.

Self Confidence: The courage that comes from certainty about our capabilities, values and goals.' (Goleman, 1998, pg. 54)

Awareness, self-assessment and confidence are important to gain a well-rounded assessment of a situation. If one of these ingredients is missing, it is difficult to make an informed decision. Emotional self-awareness is incredibly valid as it aids the decision-making process.

Bjorn Johansson, vice president of a Zurich executive search firm specialising in placing top-level executives with multinational firms, states that, 'I know within 30 seconds of meeting someone whether this person's chemistry fits with my client. Of course I need to also analyse his career, his references and the like. Still, if he doesn't pass the first barrier, my intuitive sense, I don't bother. But if my brain, heart and gut all say this is the right person, that's who I recommend.' (Goleman, 1998, pg. 53)

I find the 'first 30 seconds' test fascinating. I do strongly believe that it is a true and genuine snapshot of the person in front of you. You just know, don't you? When contributing to the recruitment and interview process, I can normally say within the first couple of minutes whether or not this person will fit the role within our school. I think it's because our brain quickly absorbs all of the information it needs and makes a quick decision about suitability. Before we've even sat down in the interview room, our brains are processing the candidate's tone of voice, the way they present themselves, whether they're humble or very loud about their successes, and whether they have a deeper knowledge of the question being asked.

What is interesting (and somewhat surprising) is that I have met and known others that don't seem to have a good sense of whether a person is genuine or not. They cannot seem to see below the surface of what is being said and instead take it all at face value. Perhaps some people do have a stronger sense of 'gut feeling' and intuition than others, or perhaps it is purely down to personal experience and what they have been through in their life, which may have developed a finely tuned intuition and self-awareness. I genuinely don't know the answer to this – I wish I did.

Empathy during a global crisis

Since I started my work on this book, the world has changed. We are all now living a 'new normal' in 'unprecedented times' – how many times have we heard that? It felt important to tailor some of my work to the current landscape, and while my thoughts and feelings are relevant for 'all times', I feel it would be remiss of me, as a reflective practitioner, not to acknowledge the here and now, and the battle we all face around coronavirus (Covid-19). Over 100,000 people have died from coronavirus in the UK, and it's likely that we have all been affected by at least one of these deaths. It is more important than ever to be mindful that we are always unaware of the internal battles and demons that another person is facing. The mantra of 'be kind' is now well known and widespread across the country, but what we really need to ensure is that the message doesn't become a throwaway hashtag, and that the meaning behind the sentiment remains at the front and centre of our practice – in the present and in the future.

The need for empathetic conversations has never been more relevant. This pandemic means that mental strength is needed in abundance as well as physical strength, and school leaders and staff are living and breathing this, day in and day out.

Providing emotional support and ongoing encouragement for parents is part of our daily 'to do' list now. I am having to say, through much of my correspondence with families, that it is OK to put their mental health first. This is often more important than learning and academic progress. And at times like this, it definitely is.

There are many headteachers around the country who are having to deal with decisions unlike any others they've ever faced. It's not just about when a deadline is met anymore or sticking to the school development plan; it's about protecting people's lives and the lives of their families. I'm not sure this was ever mentioned in any previous teacher training courses. Headteachers and senior leaders are now 'trained' in all matters Covid-19 – testing, tracking, tracing and risk assessing – to ensure that the school community is as 'Covid-secure' as possible. It has become the unthinkable. It is also unsustainable.

In the early weeks of the pandemic, one of my friends mentioned that they had been watching a TV series called *Pandemic* (March, 2020) and had finished watching a week before all of the schools closed. People often watch these types of drama on TV because they are far-fetched fantasy; it's assumed that these events wouldn't happen in our real lives. But when the TV drama takes a front seat in our lives, that's when the confusion and surrealism start to hit home.

I still remember when we had sent all of the children home, ready to begin their remote learning. I walked very slowly to the staffroom, poured myself a coffee and sat in the empty space, trying to get my head around the quick turn of events. Without sounding too dramatic, it felt like the apocalypse.

I had to stay at home to undertake the 12 weeks' shielding process during the first lockdown, as I am asthmatic. This was a hard pill for me to swallow as I live for my work, and not being able to help out in school made me feel pretty useless. My headteacher was fully supportive and she has handled this whole unprecedented scenario with grace, empathy and humility – something I would hope if I was ever put in a similar situation I'd be able to show too.

I was proactive with working from home, but when you are not working with people, seeing their enthusiasm, getting stuck into learning and seeing how proud they are at the moment of finishing their hard work, it doesn't seem as rewarding. I missed the company, my colleagues, my pupils – and yes, the banter! The face of education has changed for a while, and I for one didn't realise how at home I was in the classroom. I missed my class unbelievably, and as much as I love family life and spending time with my little girl, I felt like half of me was missing – slightly dramatic, but actually very true.

The sudden 'hard stop' of face-to-face interaction has had a very profound effect on people. I know it has on me. I'm naturally a deep thinker; anyone that knows me well knows this to be true. I have always kept myself busy as a coping strategy, and I recognise that. Having in-depth conversations with others makes me overthink less, and having a classroom of children to motivate and encourage keeps my busy mind active and positive. There is now a very real 'void' in my life, in my mind, and sometimes this can be tough to accept and overcome. How many other educators have had this same experience? I think being an educator and an 'over thinker' can sometimes go hand in hand. If Twitter is anything to go by, this seems to be true. Look back at the school holidays and see how many educators get into all sorts of debates and arguments (or 'pile ons' as they call them!) because their minds are suddenly free from school, the curriculum and pupils for a week or two. In the absence of school, they need to fill their busy and enquiring minds. It is so important that conversations, whether on social media or face to face, are handled with a strong sense of empathy. We are dealing with humans – feelings must always come first.

Be kind, right?

Thought capsule

How we treat others can change their work ethic and their thought process, and most importantly this treatment stays with a person for a long time. It is important to get it right. Trust, kindness and understanding, always.

3
Communication

It may seem strange to start a chapter about communication with the topic of silence, but…

Imagine you are in a staff meeting and a very vocal member of staff has said something quite direct and awkward, which in turn has stunned everyone into silence. The silence is almost loud, isn't it? So many questions that want to be aired, but everyone stays silent.

Notice the silence.

What is it telling us?

Silence is its own language after all.

There is almost a loud buzz of thought behind that silence.

I know from a personal point of view that when I become quiet, I am thinking deeply and have many thoughts circulating in my busy mind. Of course, the act of silence contains a multitude of different meanings for different people. Some people may well choose to be silent and are absolutely comfortable in doing so. It may well be their most natural behaviour.

It's when the silence becomes full of unsaid words that it becomes a problem. The silence can become almost toxic and can spill into the shadowy corners of the corridor, turning the school culture into a sour state of affairs.

As well as noticing communication or lack thereof, it is important to notice each other's body language, as much of our communication is through our body language. As Goleman states, 'One rule of thumb used in communications research is that 90 percent or more of an emotional message is nonverbal' (Goleman, 1995, pg. 97). I consider this to be such an important reminder when thinking about how we view communication in schools – how we 'non-verbally' communicate with colleagues, with ourselves, with parents and, of course, with the students. I find that if a parent knows that you are emotionally invested in their child, difficult situations can be ironed out quickly because you've already carved out a long-standing relationship built through consistency and communication. It's as much about what is not said as what is said.

The same can be said of the relationships between staff. If your colleagues know that you 'have their back' and you genuinely care about how they feel, then any disagreements that arise will be discussed in a respectful and understanding manner.

Vibes – more than a feeling?

When I have previously visited schools, either for a walk round before the interview or for staff meetings/moderation meetings and so on, I always take in the 'vibes' of the place. I am aware that this sounds slightly naive; however, the energy inside the building offers many signals. The energy I am referring to is from the people inside the school.

Some people are more aware of this than others. Naturally, what you have experienced in life can affect how sensitive you are to new situations; having an open mind to consider that all may not be as it seems is not something that comes easily to everyone.

As you step inside your school building, consider these questions:

- Is there an open and transparent 'trusting' energy?
- Do staff feel at ease with one other?
- Are staff productively busy?
- Are there noticeable 'groups' of people in separate areas of the school building?
- Are doors closed or open?

These are just a few killer questions. There may be other thoughts and feelings that you can't quite put into words, as they come from your gut instinct. Of course, the answers to all of these questions will depend on a range of factors, including the time you choose to visit.

I've walked into school buildings for a look around prior to interview and decided a strong 'no' or 'yes' within several seconds. Perhaps I judge too quickly, and perhaps I should wait before making a judgement. I think it's important to say here that I am open to being convinced otherwise; I just seem to make initial very quick judgements, but of course I am open to being wrong.

It is important to note that a school building can feel exceptionally calm at first glance, before you delve into the 'unspoken language' of the school culture. Equally, the opposite can be true. The building may deliver vibes of chaos and have an unsettled nature, but staff are exceptionally happy. Each school culture has its own quirks and nuances.

Unspoken language

What I mean by the 'unspoken language' of the school culture is the silent power struggles, the silent obstacles and, more positively, the silent productivity of school staff. It is only when you get to understand the dynamics of a school that these concepts and realities start to reveal themselves. I often find it fascinating to observe and learn about the 'behind the scenes' of school life. As I start to find out more about a school's 'culture', I do often wonder, 'Shouldn't it be as transparent on the inside as it is on the outside?' – within reason (GDPR regulations and the like). But, actually, could it be a positive that each school has hidden, sometimes very meaningful, quirks and a multitude of layers that make it unique? I think so.

To develop a culture where the energy matches both the spoken and unspoken conversations does take time, but it is completely worth it. Keeping emotional intelligence at the forefront of everyday educational practice is key because it develops transparent and trusting relationships between staff, parents and children, ultimately making sure that what you see is what you get, in the majority of interactions and circumstances.

Non-verbal cues

Action is just as valid, if not more important, than spoken word.

'People's emotions are rarely put into words; far more often they are expressed through other cues. The key to intuiting another's feeling is in the ability to read nonverbal channels: tone of voice, gesture, facial expression and the like.' (Goleman, 1995, pg. 96)

As Goleman suggests, there is a lot to be said for reading non-verbal cues. I am sure you are familiar with the phrase 'silence speaks louder than words'.

I have always considered body language and non-verbal cues to have a greater importance than what is actually said. My gut instincts, the signals I've received subconsciously, tell me most of what I need to know, especially when taking part in the interview process. It is the little details you notice that hold significance. Having a strong sense of emotional intelligence ensures that you pick up on the little alarm signals and respond to them effectively.

'Just as the mode of the rational mind is words, the mode of emotions is nonverbal. Indeed, when a person's words disagree with what is conveyed via his/her tone of voice, gesture or nonverbal channel, the emotional truth is in the way he/she says something rather than what is said.' (Goleman, 1995, pp. 96–97)

I think, on reflection, I notice the little signals because beneath the tough skin of leadership I am a sensitive person and I tend to see traits of similar sensitivities in others. I don't consider this sensitivity a weakness; I see it as a strength. Being sensitive often means you are a deep thinker and so you tend to be aware of how others could be feeling and take this into account.

Here's an example of being aware of non-verbal cues that I remember very clearly from a scenario when I was in Year 8 at secondary school: I put lots of effort into a religious education project and received an A grade as a result. As I received this result in an envelope, I spotted that the boy sitting next to me was disappointed (facial expression) with his result, and so I quickly put mine back in the envelope and asked him (considerately) about his project. I was so very aware of how he would feel if I was to celebrate my result, while he sat there bitterly disappointed with his.

Responding to non-verbal cues

I've always been very aware of how people are feeling and have a tendency to notice the little changes in people's behaviour, even when subtle. 'The noticing business is a simple but profound way of improving practice at every level within an organisation. It gives people power, good power which they don't abuse because they have been trusted. It distinguishes the person from the work, so that nothing becomes personal. Thus, if someone is praised, they don't become big headed, because they know that good work is produced through their efforts.' (Myatt, 2016, pg. 88) Mary Myatt refers to noticing the little details as 'the noticing business', which is fundamental to the success of a school culture. After all, it is the little things that mean a lot.

As a teacher and leader, now and again I have to remind myself that comments are not personal and that you cannot control how another person chooses to react to what is said. What you can control, however, is how you respond and how well you embrace the situation while maintaining your integrity. This doesn't mean lacking empathy or giving the situation the cold shoulder – quite the opposite: it means that you stay calm, considered and show empathy when that person needs to be consoled. An example of this is that you may say something genuinely and someone else takes it the wrong way and takes offence: a leader says, 'I'm going to trust you on this one', thinking they are providing positivity and trust, but in actual fact all their colleague heard was a lack of trust, and then they ended up mistakenly thinking, 'So you didn't trust me before?'.

Treating others with respect, dignity and compassion should be the core foundation of all teaching and leadership styles. I'm sure (and I hope) many of you will agree.

I have always searched for this notion in previous senior leadership teams and, to be honest, examples that I've seen have been few and far between. I've spent quite a number of years just observing, and thinking to myself, 'Would I have dealt with that situation in that way?' Very often the answer has been 'absolutely not!'

In order to build your resilience, it is important not to shy away from difficult conversations, even if you find them as difficult as I do. I have had to throw myself in at the deep end and offer to have these conversations to ensure I am building my resilience, but also so that I have a heightened understanding of the way in which people can respond. I always listen carefully and if I need to apologise, I will do. But what I won't do is change the content of the difficult conversation because, unfortunately, this has to stick. The more you understand your colleagues and learn what makes them tick, the easier it can be to have these conversations.

Headstrong *and* humble?

Are you headstrong but humble? By this I mean are your core values and beliefs unshakable, but you are willing to listen, be empathetic and make decisions with an open mind? In my opinion, being headstrong is having the determination to listen to your gut instinct and make decisions you think are best for others. It also means that you are stubborn, which I view as a positive trait. The reason I say this is because in teaching you need to be a little stubborn:

Stubborn – to not give up and to get the best out of a child.
Stubborn – to continue working towards a set goal, even when you feel like giving up.
Stubborn – to push yourself that little bit harder when you know you need to achieve your best.

Normally the word 'stubborn' is viewed negatively, but perhaps we need to change the narrative? Stubbornness is only negative when you don't take on board other people's viewpoints. I think in teaching and in leadership you need to have a certain 'stubbornness' to achieve what is best for the children. Be headstrong enough to trust your decisions but humble enough to adapt when needed.

Ego – the loud versus the quiet

I'm sure we will all agree that there is some degree of 'ego' within everyone's personality. This comes into play and can be quite reactive within a school environment, or any working environment for that matter.

Ego plays a large part in how we view challenges and questions about our authority. When someone allows their ego to play a leading role in conversations, questions from another person can be seen as a challenge to the ego. In fact, the other person may simply want to gain an insight into your thinking and be completely genuine. An individual who doesn't place their ego to one side may well assume that any questions undermine their views, when really they are being asked to clarify and work alongside that person. Simply changing your perspective on questions can change your behaviour.

For people who have had to deal with difficult situations, their ego can act almost as a protective barrier to prevent them from getting hurt by actions, situations and words. This makes ego a tricky concept to reflect on. However, most will recognise that it takes strength to be vulnerable, to admit when you are wrong and to hold your hands up and say, 'I'm sorry; I hear you'. This is not to say that you don't feel agitated or frustrated by a situation, but it is openly telling the other person, 'I'm sorry; your feelings are important'.

In work situations, I place logical thinking above my emotions; it's a case of mind over matter. I realise that the way someone reacts in a given situation is very much an emotional response that probably has very little to do with what has been said, but more to do with dormant emotions that have suddenly been stirred. Having worked with a range of different people I am very much beginning to see that everyone is so very different. Our brains have meandered their way through life attaching a vast range of emotions to events; no two people's paths are the same. I see this as a positive. It helps each of us gain a wider perspective and learn to appreciate what others have to offer. In order to appreciate differences and keep an open mind, it's important to place our egos on the back burner.

An ego can be secure but silent. It's possible to have 'an ego so secure it doesn't need to be put on display. An ego which is so secure that it is not rocked by petty criticism. An ego which provides a quiet moral compass and purpose.' (Myatt, 2016, pg. 94) A true and genuine teacher and leader is humble about what has been achieved; they know they have worked hard and put their all into their work. They don't expect compliments but welcome them warmly if they arrive. People who remain humble and are hardworking are the people you would want to work alongside.

It doesn't bode well when a teacher or leader has an egotistical nature as they are unlikely to see (or want to see) how other people are feeling. In the case of a leader, pride must be swallowed in order for staff to see the leader first and foremost as a human. Another point to mention here is that 'behaviour breeds behaviour' and so, in cases where the leadership is overly egotistical, the school culture will be full of staff that want to communicate but are too afraid to do so. This isn't healthy and this is when creativity, autonomy and emotions are stifled.

When a leader chooses to be open-minded and allow their actions to match their words, staff will positively respond. As humans we are naturally inclined to trust what others say and we like to remain hopeful. However, when that trust is destroyed, it takes a very long time to build it back up.

I have witnessed leaders that shout louder than anyone else because they believe in the power of control. This does not win hearts and minds. Staff will do as they are told to, as there is no other option – but it will be a robotic response. Creativity, passion and enthusiasm to trial new ways of teaching, learning and building a school culture will be lost. By behaving in this way, this type of leader has booked themselves a one-way ticket to a never-ending interviewing process, as staff will come and go because they know that they are viewed as replaceable and are therefore not valued.

Quiet confusion and control

I've found that leaders who don't 'check in' with their staff often find that the distance and silence between themselves and their staff cause distrust and confusion; words that need to be spoken are left unspoken. Staying quiet and not letting someone know where they stand can be confusing for people, especially if communication is important to them.

Can a silent and observant teacher or leader also be emotionally intelligent? Of course! There are many quiet leaders who are fantastic at tapping into their emotional intelligence. However, it is vital to remain vigilant to the following possibilities: someone may be silent because they are out of their depth or they may be silent because they are manipulative. It is this second type of leader we need to be wary of.

I have been quite naive and oblivious to quiet control in the past and have automatically assumed that leaders who are quiet are emotionally intelligent. I wrongly assumed that those who are quiet are always reflecting and carefully thinking through scenarios; unfortunately, this isn't always the case. For some, a lack of empathy and an ability to remain calm and show no emotion may be purely because they don't consider emotional intelligence to be a valid part of their role.

It is important to recognise this quickly in order to be free of that type of control that a leader may try to have over you. As negative and cynical as this viewpoint sounds (which is why it took me a while to realise), it's quite significant. I've had first-hand experiences of leaders using emotional intelligence to quietly control, something I naively took as 'they are quiet, because they are observing', when in actual fact they were busy calculating their next move. I always tend to see the good in people and therefore possibly, subconsciously, I didn't examine their behaviour effectively enough until I was caught off guard.

I'm not suggesting that you should over-analyse when a leader is quiet, as it may just be their nature, but I would very much consider your gut instincts and any warning flags that catch you off guard. Keep those scenarios metaphorically 'logged' if you feel uneasy about them.

As a cautionary word, if a leader has a quiet approach it may be necessary for you to learn to live with their calm and silent leadership style – with an open mind first and foremost because, as suggested previously, the likelihood is that it is just their personality. Introverted leaders are very often among the most effective leaders.

Let's consider the flip side of this: could we suggest that a bold, direct and loud leadership style uses little emotional intelligence? What assumptions could be made and how accurate are these assumptions? I put this question to Drew Povey, leadership consultant and former headteacher. This is what he said:

'This is a great question and my view is that the emotionally intelligent leader can adapt their behaviour to meet the needs of the person they are working with. This may mean they are quiet at times and bold and direct at others. I also feel that we must measure this by the impact and influence they possess with others. I agree that there are too many assumptions made in this arena, particularly in the field of coaching, but if a leader can be situational (which takes emotional intelligence to read correctly) and can influence people positively, then the impact is priceless.'

Diplomatic communication with parents

Having diplomatic conversations, being flexible and understanding that everyone has different ways of expressing how they feel are vital to our role as teachers and leaders. It's up to us to absorb the situation, listen intently and be open to how others feel, despite previous judgements or how you feel about the situation in front of you.

Allowing parents to come to you and remaining open to suggestions when they do, rather than being closed off and defensive, is a skill to be mastered. The majority of the time, parents have their own and their child/children's emotional wellbeing at the forefront of their minds and so this needs to be addressed. Some educators see responding quickly to parental suggestions as weak, but I would suggest that it is a strength because working together is the best solution for both children and the parents. It allows parents to be understood and it also strengthens a teacher's knowledge of that child and their parents. What are their specific needs and wants?

Another key feature of communicating with parents is understanding that parents can become angry and frustrated, and everyone presents their anger in different ways. If a parent approaches you in anger or becomes angry, the best thing to do is to listen and to absorb. In the heat of the moment, offer no defence, no matching of their levels of anger; instead, offer calmness and clarity and take in the information they are presenting to you. Sometimes people just need to let their thoughts be aired and then, once they have done this, changes are made, advice is taken on board and we move forward.

You may feel a range of different emotions while a parent airs their frustration to you, but in order to make headway and resolve the situation quickly and calmly, sometimes it is best to just stand and listen. Other colleagues may feel this is weak, because they think this is 'giving in' or 'giving too much time to a situation'. Let them feel that way – let them vent their own frustrations – but also know that you are showing strong, sustainable and adaptable impact. It is only the teachers and leaders who possess a deeper understanding of the 'why' who will understand precisely why you are putting in this effort. Parents can see that you have a strong desire to do 'the right thing' and children can visibly see that you are working with, rather than against, their parent(s). I am not suggesting you make changes at the drop of a hat, or if the situation doesn't require change just yet, but it's about hearing those situations that have grounding, being open to seeing others' perspectives and reasons and realising that – yes – there are many times when parents can raise genuine concerns or suggestions for improvement and these will require action.

⋅ Gaining people's trust, especially the trust of parents, takes time. But once they see consistent efforts, communication and changes made, that trust starts to develop, and it means that when there is a tricky situation that you need to discuss, then this will inherently be less challenging because you have already built the foundations.

As we know, the relationship between parents and teachers holds significant importance. Here is a case study and discussion from Anoara Mughal, a Year 6 teacher and member of SLT, who discusses how important the relationship between teachers and parents is.

Anoara Mughal, member of SLT and Year 6 teacher

There is no doubt that maintaining positive relationships with parents is key to pupils doing well at school. According to the Education Endowment Foundation (EEF) (2021), the parental role and the degree to which parents engage with school determines academic outcomes. This is where schools can come into their own and engage parents in a variety of ways such as:

- providing regular feedback on children's progress
- offering advice on improving the home learning environment
- running more intensive programmes for children struggling with reading or behaviour.

Self-awareness is having a deep understanding of one's own emotions, weaknesses and areas of strength. This includes recognition of our own values and goals and using gut feelings to guide decisions, while realising their own impact on others. Self-regulation is the ability to control one's emotions and impulses and change or redirect emotions, according to the situation. Social skills are required to manage other people's emotions in the direction required. When making decisions, it is important to consider the feelings of others; this is empathy. Motivation is required to achieve the desired outcome or goal.

Goleman (2000a) suggests that these learned capabilities can be developed over time, which will lead to outstanding performance. Although emotional intelligence is not recognised as being a crucial factor in learning yet, in the business world it is considered to be extremely useful.

Our emotions can become overwhelmed or flooded during times of extreme stress. Being able to recognise and understand our emotions, as well as those of others, and simultaneously regulating them appropriately prevents the fight or flight response.

In society, having emotional intelligence can be perceived as a gaping weakness. Keeping quiet about issues or not standing up for yourself can be interpreted as plain ignorance. Why would some think that it is a weakness, while others consider this a strength?

Throughout my teaching career and prior to becoming a teacher, I have witnessed many great examples of managing one's own emotional responses to situations. As a teacher and school leader, I also have witnessed the impact of managing one's own emotional responses, where the person in question has not only been able to manage their own feelings about a situation but has also been adept at managing the feelings of the other person. Needless to say, there have been other times when perhaps managing one's emotions would have been more appropriate to prevent a situation from escalating.

There was a particular incident where a teacher, who had been returning to full-time work after a brief part-time stint, was placed in a Year 3 class. At the time, the assistant headteacher (AHT), who was also the Year 3 class teacher, was stepping up to being the acting deputy headteacher (DHT), and so the school required a full-time Year 3 teacher.

The situation was ideal for both the school and for the returning teacher. Understandably, some parents were not happy about a sudden change in teacher mid-way through the year. One of the parents, who was a challenge to engage, put in a complaint about the new teacher. The acting DHT arranged a meeting between the three of them to ascertain what the issues were, and to provide an opportunity to air them and to resolve them.

First the issues of handwriting and spellings were brought up. The teacher calmly explained the school policies on these two important areas and the challenges that the pupil faced.

Then the issue about not engaging with the parent was brought up and the parent was given the time to explore and explain feelings of being ignored. The teacher could have argued back and explained the challenges involved in engaging parents but instead decided to apologise to the parent.

Finally, the parent brought up the fact that they had been told that the teacher was outstanding but that clearly he was not. This was a particularly emotionally charged situation for the teacher, having put everything into his career; this one statement could have been destructive for both parties involved.

It would be natural to become defensive – after all, teachers work extremely hard and this felt like a personal attack. Instead of taking the comment personally, the teacher calmly apologised for what the parent was thinking and stated the steps he had taken to improve the child's learning.

The parent left the meeting in a calm manner, feeling reassured that his child was being looked after and that his child's learning needs were being catered for.

The teacher's colleagues thought he should have stood up for himself but he did not agree with this. Take a moment to reflect on your own thoughts and feelings about this situation. Consider the following questions:

- Should the teacher have apologised?
- Was it a mistake to apologise?
- How did he manage to contain himself and his emotions?
- How did he simultaneously manage his own emotions and those of the parent?
- What events or training experiences may have led to such control of emotions?

Impact on parents

In the situation just described, the parent immediately relaxed when the teacher apologised. Apologising levelled the playing field and ensured that instead of one person having the upper hand, both were speaking on equal terms. There may have been an air of uncertainty and fear rippling through the community, with a new teacher taking a class in the middle of an academic year. Being able to manage the teacher's own emotions as well as the parent's meant that the parent left feeling positive and would have passed on the messages of positivity throughout the community, thereby instilling positive beliefs. In addition to this, another positive impact was that the parent felt more confident in engaging with the school.

Impact on pupils

Although the children never knew about this situation, apologising meant that the parent left satisfied that his views had been heard and considered. This message was then passed through the community and this ripple of positivity would have a huge impact on how children viewed their own teachers.

Impact on staff

Modelling the use of emotional intelligence to staff can be very powerful. Talking about it afterwards and explaining the thought processes can have a positive impact beyond the immediate situation. This enables others to learn about their own self-efficacy and self-regulation, particularly during challenging times. In turn, this enables them to manage their own emotions. It helps to develop an awareness and understanding of those around you, which in turn leads to continued beneficial actions and interactions.

We do not know what the future holds but as the world continues to grapple with Covid-19 and its impact, there is no doubt that our attentions should be turned towards developing emotional intelligence and resilience to enable our pupils to navigate their way through an increasingly complex and ever-changing world.

A dynamic classroom

I've had to learn quickly as I've been faced with plenty of challenges in the classroom and, to be honest, I haven't minded learning this way. There is something to be said for being thrown in at the deep end – you have to absorb information and act rather quickly. It doesn't work for everyone as, of course, everyone learns differently, but it has worked for me.

There is always going to be a multitude of characters in a classroom and that is the way it should be. Everyone is different. That is what makes classroom life both thoroughly enjoyable and, at times, equally exhausting. Some behaviours take time to fully understand and others lend themselves to new classroom routines and structures. As a person, I find it very rewarding when you've worked with a child for a long period of time and you understand their quirks, their communication, their humour and the way they work. Many of these children cannot simply change the way they behave; it is embedded, it is part of who they are. If you are asking a child with special educational needs to change their behaviour, that is like asking them to change their genetic make-up – which, as you know, is impossible. Instead, you need to work with what you have and you need to remain empathetic to the fact that, yes, a child may do wrong and, yes, their behaviour may be problematic, but they are still a child that needs care, consideration and patience.

I wish all parents understood and could see how empathetic and caring children are towards one another in the classroom, because I don't think they fully understand the impact of their words at times. I've lost count of the amounts of times a child has said to me, 'But Mrs CR, I can't play with this child because I'm not allowed to.' It's truly heartbreaking. These are children! We spend a large proportion of our time teaching children to be accepting of each other, as we are all very different. To have this culture pulled apart by the seams at home is truly difficult to hear. Of course, there will be times where children are advised to keep their distance due to social issues and minor disagreements, but to be told you cannot spend time with another person because they are different is just not kind or fair.

I asked Johnathan Lear (author of *The Monkey-Proof Box*, 2019) what he considers to be the most important strand of emotional intelligence within teaching. Here's his response: 'Empathy would be right up there – the teacher who doesn't just write off a child as being badly behaved, but takes the time to work out why – to build a supportive relationship.'

Each class I've ever taught has had a range of SEND, but I am pleased I've had this opportunity to work with and understand those with complex needs. It's given me a deep-rooted understanding of what is important to these children, how they navigate their way through life and how unique and special they really are. Other children are naturally caring towards those who have difficulties – you can't teach this; it is just present.

Just as you can't teach that natural empathy and curiosity that children display, you cannot teach an adult to understand – even with countless CPD sessions about awareness involving special needs. They may well take on the information and process it, but you find that only a few (who are dedicated and passionate) put it into daily action. There are educators that may want to learn, but do not seek to understand. They may allow their cognitive bias to navigate their response to difficult situations rather than their newly acquired knowledge and desire to understand. You can lead a horse to water, but you cannot make it drink.

A calm approach

When a member of staff comes to you with a difficult situation and you react in a calm, considered way (which is needed), some may feel frustrated or that you haven't dealt with the situation. It's almost as though they feel like the situation hasn't been dealt with (properly) because the response wasn't fury, drama or strong words. I strongly believe these types of responses often add fuel to the fire, and acting directly from emotion is something that should be steered clear of at all times.

There is much to be said for unspoken, subtle responses – but how do others, who cannot sense these little actions, see what you have achieved? It can be difficult to explain to someone the 'why' in this case when their emotional intelligence and awareness is on a completely different level.

I've witnessed many scenarios whereby a situation has occurred and it has been resolved well with both staff members and children feeling calm and with the positive perspective that tomorrow will very much be a new day. As a leader, you feel that all avenues have been investigated and understood and the situation is in the best place it can be. However, this does not stop others from casting their opinions, doubt and influence over the situation. You have to learn to stick to your guns and remain quietly confident that everything was handled in the best possible way. If you respond to comments and opinions, you are outwardly justifying your actions, but the very fact that all parties (including parents) were happy with how the situation was dealt with speaks volumes.

Actions sometimes really do speak louder than words. At times like these, words don't hold much weight.

There is a lot to be said for quiet, calm leadership. Of course, communication is vital and that is very much top of the list, but quiet, intentional action and vision is what it all comes down to. 'It's the careful and deliberate consideration of what makes a school work; and in the classroom, what supports deep learning, both for teachers and learners.' (Myatt, 2016, pg. 23)

The teachers and leaders that sit with an idea a little longer and think carefully are often the ones who make strong decisions, but that is not to say that leaders who work in different and equally effective ways have less of an impact. We have all experienced and seen strong and weak leadership for a multitude of reasons.

Thought capsule

Mutual respect, care, shared values and an understanding of where a person is in their career are so important. This is being able to meet others where they are. Acknowledge that sometimes it is best just to listen and say 'I hear you' in order to build strong relationships and to build bridges when times get tough.

4
Toolbox

In this chapter, we will start to explore all of the 'tools' that an emotionally intelligent professional can have at their disposal in their emotional intelligence toolbox.

We will discuss how the timing of a particular conversation can have a huge impact on how the message is received and, most importantly, on how well the request, task or demand is executed.

We will take a look at the importance of understanding that 'school' is only one aspect of a person's life, and that very often we will know very little about what is going on in their 'real world'. An understanding of an individual's circumstances, both in school and in their private life, is crucial in order to ensure that your words and messages are not only heard but also listened to and acted upon as you would have hoped them to be.

We will look at the quandary that is as old as time itself – should you be led by your heart or your head? – as headteacher Flora Cooper poses a number of important questions.

Finally, we will examine a number of other tools that we can have at our disposal, such as self-awareness, and see the effect of these handy tools in practice in a fascinating case study by assistant headteacher Scott Wellington. Scott describes the impact of the 'emotionally intelligent toolbox' across his school's setting, and it is a truly captivating read.

It's all about timing

Knowing how to lead your team effectively while keeping their emotional wellbeing at the forefront of everything you do should be a priority. Fully understanding and taking responsibility for what keeps people afloat within a sea of seemingly never-ending work-related tasks is difficult to manage, but it should be the aspiration of every leader.

> Think before acting. Can a certain task wait until the next day? Does it have to be executed immediately? Will it benefit certain members of staff if you wait to act?

Quality over quantity at all times

If several projects and CPD are pursued all at once, the focus is lost, motivation is dampened and the person undertaking the projects will feel unnecessarily overwhelmed. Quiet, intentional change happens when information, development and subtle nudges in the right direction are done at the right time and when this is 'reinforced by leaders who understand the importance of "fewer things in greater depth" which comes from "digging deeper and lingering longer"'. (Myatt, 2016, pg. 26)

As teachers, experience teaches us when to intervene at the right time. We always look out for opportunities to strengthen connections in learning and praise effort, to enforce a love of learning. Leaders encouraging colleagues should mirror what we see in the classroom and know the correct time to implement change and push learning. Too much too soon, or in quick succession, can cause fatigue among colleagues. A new idea or intervention needs to be embedded enough for the staff to 'enjoy' its positive impact before being set off in the direction of a shiny new idea. Constant lurching from intervention to intervention, chasing an outcome, is all too often found in schools desperately seeking improvement (perhaps from an Ofsted category), and the desire to find the 'silver bullet' is real. Change happens in stages. Alice and David Kolb's *The Experiential Educator* (2017) outlines why it is important to let changes become embedded before jumping onto the next fad – hands up who remembers 'thinking hats' and 'talk partners'!

As a leader, it is important to understand exactly where your staff are, both professionally and personally. Conversely, as a teacher, it is important to know that your leadership team are there for support if and when you need them. This support allows teachers to blossom in the best way that they can.

Leaders shouldn't just be pushing staff forward onto the next project, with little thought for their wellbeing. Leaders need to consider that it may not be the right time for them. Address progression when the time is right; the focus may be in another, more important area for a while. This type of leadership requires patience and understanding, but also knowledge that if development is pursued at the wrong time, then it will amount to nothing. The person in question will not put their attention and effort in if the timing is off, so it will be lost time and a waste of resources.

Choose carefully when to disseminate information to staff and always take on board how busy their workload is at that specific time and, more importantly, how others are coping with high demand. There may be a member of staff who is sailing through the workload and completely taking it in their stride, but you may also have another member of staff with the same workload who is really struggling and perhaps not asking for support due to the fear of letting you down. You may have strong characters in your team, but equally you may have vulnerability. It is vital to keep an eye on both, as dynamics within a team are everything. The best team is made up of the sum of its individual parts; a team of colleagues with the same skills, knowledge and understanding is not as strong as a group of people coming together and bringing with them their individual and unique talents, focusing on a shared and common goal. There will be strong characters, and there will be vulnerability among others, but here's a takeaway thought: does that mean someone can't be vulnerable *and* strong? I'll leave that with you for a moment.

Don't act on several different sources at the same time. Take one focus, work on it and make sure it's of good quality. We don't over-complicate tasks for the children we teach; let's use the same structure for the adults we work with.

Reading signals

Accuracy and knowing the correct time to have a conversation or check in on a colleague are important. If you choose the wrong timing (too soon) they could be overwhelmed and not be able to take on your support or understanding. Some people prefer to deal with situations alone and there is nothing wrong with that – it is up to the leader or colleague to decipher that this is the best port of call. I prefer to work through problems alone, as then I have the headspace to think every option through, while others prefer to discuss options; both are equally effective and it is down to the individual and how they operate.

Timing your interventions is also relevant when dealing with disputes between children and having difficult conversations with parents. Read their signals and wait if needed. Well-grounded and considered solutions take time to develop – quick solutions only provide a sticking plaster for a short time, before the wound gets knocked and opened again.

It is our intuition that tells us when quick action is needed. In his 2019 book *The Wellbeing Toolkit*, Andrew Cowley states that 'our empathy kit relates to the speed of thought and can be seen in sport. For every sharp catch in the slips or impeccably timed run and volley into the top corner, there will be a mistimed passing shot or long misplaced pass into acres of the wrong space. Quick reactions can turn a result; it is the equivalent quick reactions that enable us to diffuse the trickiest situations in our classrooms and in conflicts between children and between parents.' (Cowley, 2019, pg. 52)

Cowley quite rightly points out that some situations need attention immediately to ensure that the tension is diffused – but it's about knowing which situations they are. It's about prioritising and putting out the flames before the heat causes damage.

Before having difficult conversations or feeding information to staff, consider these questions:

- Have I considered how the other person is feeling at that moment in time?
- Is there a situation in their personal life that could affect their processing skills?
- Are they exhausted, anxious or on edge due to workload?

Once this has been reflected upon, then consider how that individual tends to work:

- What does this person thrive on?
- What is most likely to ensure that they are enthusiastic and feel happy about the task in hand?
- Are they a perfectionist and do they want to alter plans to suit their individual working style?

The main reason for these reflections, of course, is to ensure that the team remains positive, motivated and proactive. Once something is said or received in the wrong way, it can be difficult to rewind, as opinions and judgements have already been formed. I always think of the screwed-up paper metaphor: once you have screwed up a piece of paper into a ball, trying to smooth out all of the creases is impossible. You cannot revert back to that smooth piece of paper; the damage has been done. The same can be said of words. There is no editing tool to use once those words have left your mouth, and the effect those words can have on someone can be irreversible.

> Adapt to the signals you are given. To get the best out of each individual, you need to listen to their way of working, as this will ultimately contribute to a stronger result.

Life beyond the school gate

I think it is so important to note that someone at work may appear fine but you have absolutely no idea what is going on in their home lives. You have no idea. None. Unless, of course, they choose to share that information with you.

'Men and women are more than their work. They have a life beyond the confines of the daily nine to five. They have the joys and sadness which are the lot of every human being. While they might be put on hold when at work, they are still there in the background, bubbling away.' (Myatt, 2016, pg. 14) I think everyone has the capacity to hold a double persona, and so how they are in the workplace may be completely at odds with how they might act at home. On the flip side of this, they may act in a similar fashion to the way they act at home; each person has their own particular way of 'being'.

We can try our utmost to ensure that colleagues feel supported and happy, but we cannot always be responsible for when they feel unhappy. Jill Berry suggested to me that 'ensuring they remain happy' is difficult (perhaps impossible) as people's happiness is affected by a wide range of factors, many of them outside the professional context and not within our control. However, dealing with individuals with sensitivity and compassion can help them to process and face challenges and support their resilience, though not necessarily securing constant happiness. This rings true and I am learning that you cannot control another person's emotional responses (as much as it would be ideal to do so) but what you can do is control your own by staying calm, observing carefully and staying as transparent as possible.

> Each person you work with will have a home life and so emotions will vary in accordance with situations outside of work. Be aware, be considerate and remember that, as much as we would like to be, we cannot be happy all of the time.

Considering different perspectives

Working with a range of different people always brings about fresh challenges. However, these challenges are what make us more effective and dynamic within our teaching or leadership role. Something I've reflected upon and learned quite recently is that nobody has the same outlook or perspective as you. They may well have a similar ethos and work expectations, but everyone you meet has been through a range of different challenges and situations in their lifetime that have altered their thinking process. So, when you communicate with each individual in your team, it is vital that they understand your point of view, but more importantly that you understand how they have interpreted or received the information.

Previous experiences create an initial internal response/reaction. That experience causes us to react in a certain way and this internal bias could cloud our judgement and how we respond to the given situation. A key example of this is when someone has been picked up on something that they are doing incorrectly and they have previously had negative experiences (similar to this) before, which really unsettled them. They may react in anger and take one comment that is meant as a constructive improvement as a direct criticism. An emotionally intelligent leader will openly apologise if they get something wrong, but also apologise if another member of the team has misinterpreted the information, since it's possible that the leader could have been clearer or delivered the information in a more effective way.

> Perspective is so important. Unfortunately, our perspectives do have a cognitive bias and so it is important to unpick how we feel, as we may have processed a situation incorrectly. Check, review and re-evaluate.

Past experience – the amygdala remembers

People will always take information and perceive it with their inbuilt perspective. What I mean by this is that experiences that have happened in the past that have caused hurt, anger or humiliation stay with us. As much as you try to forget the experiences, they remain within our thinking, like a fight or flight mechanism. The amygdala remembers.

The amygdala is the part of our brain that recalls and associates emotions with events. It can cause the brain to have an illogical, irrational overreaction to a situation, thus causing a simple message that was completely clear to be held hostage by our amygdala and then released with several different layers of emotion added to it.

When you experience something in the present that is similar to a previous experience you have had, your mind processes the current situation and attaches past or current trauma to these experiences.

Of course, we can't always be held responsible for how others process information, but we can have a strong awareness of how we choose to use our words and our body language, and how empathetic we are to others.

If you are in an educational environment that is toxic, any negativity is felt more much strongly when fear is already embedded. Trigger points are very raw. But when you feel safe and trusted in your setting, any criticism or negativity is lessened and felt more acutely.

I try to notice how colleagues are feeling when checking in with them informally, for example during short conversations at the photocopier. In this common situation, it's possible to observe their mood and observe the way they are communicating with others.

I'm sure many teachers and leaders can sense if something is amiss within the school, as the 'communication' vibes tend to be very strong and linger in the school corridors.

Neurology

I think it's important to know and understand how the brain interprets and can respond to information around us, especially within a school setting. Our brains process a vast range of information throughout our marathon of a school day, and they do so at a very fast rate.

'When a person says an untruth, flashes of emotion appear on their face but they might only last for a few milliseconds, too fast for the human eye to detect. [...] It mirrors the expression and feeds back into the emotional circuits in your brain, causing you to gain a subtle (intuitive) feeling of how they are feeling. When you sense someone is sad, even though they are acting happy, you might be getting an accurate picture of how they really feel.' (Hamilton, 2012)

It is clear to see that our brain is a complex, multi-layered facet that sometimes retrieves information accurately depending on how an individual may be feeling. But in contrast to this, there are still many inaccuracies that may indeed be obstacles to the way we think and react to situations. It's always best to keep an open mind and be as reflective and as self-aware as we possibly can.

> Our brains are hardwired to remember situations – both good and bad. This does make communication and some situations more complex, as there are a range of different experiences brought to the table. However, if handled in the correct way, these prior thoughts and perspectives can be broken down and understood.

Relationship management

Flora Cooper, a headteacher, posed some key questions on Twitter:

- Is it better to think logically or think with the heart?
- Are there situations where one is better than the other?

Flora continues, 'I believe there are times for both, but I think many an opportunity would be missed if decisions were based purely on logical thought.' (Cooper, 2020)

I think it is important to recognise that we do often make decisions led by our heart. We consider how we feel. The mind does, of course, have an input but very often how you 'feel' about a situation dictates your next step. For example, so many teachers and leaders leave a school because of the way they were made to feel. If we were all fluent in emotional intelligence, and could use that language to ensure that those around us are made to feel valued, respected and trusted, imagine how many teaching careers could be saved! Quite often, it isn't the workload that is the issue but the workload combined with a toxic environment that pushes educators to the edge.

If you are made to feel trusted and valued to manage your own workload, then this is a different matter. The workload is still there, but you know you can complete the work without being hounded or micromanaged. This makes a significant and meaningful difference.

I've had to learn over the years that not everyone has the same open, honest and transparent way of working, which was a hard lesson to learn. I am competitive, but only with myself, so I never understood the need for others to try to push people down in order to make sure they move forward. I've seen this happen so often in schools, and the people that are pushed out are made to feel so isolated. It's awful to witness.

> Feeling trusted to do a good job goes a long, long way. Of course we have to check in and have discussions about progress and strategic changes, but if the trust is apparent then these conversations typically run smoothly, with positive outcomes.

Management plans

I once worked alongside an NQT who wasn't eating properly because they were placed on a management plan. The management plan just made the situation worse, when all the NQT needed was some good mentoring and examples of how to challenge the higher-achieving children. It was a classic example of senior management not recognising what was needed to help improve a situation.

I was asked to work alongside this NQT to provide support and, needless to say, after a couple of sessions they were flourishing and the management plan was removed. I had provided feedback to the leadership team about their progress and their eagerness to learn and improve.

The damage these management plans and various scheduled observations do to a person cannot be reversed. It stays with that person, and so any time they think they are falling below the line, their anxiety will increase because of prior experiences.

Another example of experiences that can leave a mark is having a formal observation. In one particular situation, I was ushered in to support the person being observed as they were left in floods of tears, destroyed by feedback.

Let's just reflect and go back to basic human responses for a moment. If you make another person cry, in their professional or personal life, is that person going to walk away thinking, 'Well, that was a pleasant experience, I will think carefully about how I can improve my teaching practice now'? No – undoubtedly they will walk away feeling crushed, and from then onwards they will associate every single learning walk and observation with that experience, causing that person to feel demotivated and ultimately like a failure.

What I can't get my head around is that this type of situation still happens in schools around the country. There is still a culture of 'Let's see what they can take before they break!' in some places. There are other ways to help an individual become resilient and develop a tough skin without taking them to breaking point first.

Of course everyone reacts in different ways and some will fight back, but the honest truth is that the bad experience will leave a mental scar – a scar that wasn't necessary to have in the first place!

As much as we all try to keep our emotions in check, our reactions, actions and motivations are all interconnected by emotion. Some people are better at hiding emotions and can therefore remain calm and have less of an emotional reaction to situations inside of school, but there will always be members of staff who find it difficult to keep their emotions in check, for many different reasons, but probably the most common being because they are so passionate about their work. It's about teaching and modelling to those people that you can still be passionate and proactive without responding to every situation emotionally, as this takes up far too much energy, especially when you are working with children on a day-to-day basis.

Finding the right words when emotions are running high can be difficult and very often the wrong words are chosen. This can put the person on the defensive and, most importantly, this person will remember that interaction because it sparked an emotional response.

An emotionally intelligent person will look beyond the way someone is choosing to behave to establish why they are behaving in this way. There will always be a reason, a reaction, a trigger point, something so miniscule that may well, having been left unaddressed, have become a much larger problem. If we remember that we are humans first and professionals second then we can also remember that, regardless of what some professionals believe, we do use our emotions first and foremost.

Our emotional compass filters through every little thing we say and do. For example, if you receive a challenging email, your first response may be anger, followed swiftly by the calm yet indignant decision to 'put the world and this person to rights'. Or perhaps, if the subject of the email has made you feel fearful, then a barrage of anxious thoughts may follow. Both reactions are very much emotion-led. As teachers and leaders, we may have mastered the fine-tuned art of regulating our emotions in the workplace, but that doesn't mean that the brain is able to switch off the neurological reminders of how a situation makes you feel. Regulation is necessary but what is a real shame is that we can't erase how a previous situation has made us feel; that stays stored in our amygdala to remind us of past feelings while in a similar situation.

Management plans! Why not work alongside a person to build their confidence? When someone is struggling, handing them a management plan, or something similar, will completely crush them. Support them, don't crucify them.

Self-awareness and other useful tools

I asked a few educators the following question:

What aspect of emotional intelligence do you see as vital to succeed as a teacher and a leader?

Drew Povey, education consultant and former headteacher, responded to this question:

'I would say that self-awareness is the key element for teachers and leaders. Without this, very little can be built on, without such a foundation. Only when we are truly aware of how we operate and how this impacts others, can we truly connect with people. I also believe that self-awareness is crucial for leaders to "know themselves" better. It's not until we have an understanding of what our world views are, where our biases lie and the things that can trigger us (see Goldsmith and Reiter's (2015) book, *Triggers: Sparking positive change and making it last*) can we really lead properly.'

As Povey suggests, you need to leave your biases behind and lead without letting your emotions be triggered. This can prove a challenge, but is a worthwhile lesson to learn. *How can we leave our biases behind?* This is done by closely questioning our initial thoughts… Where have they come from? Why have they been formed?

Sam Strickland, principal of The Duston School, suggests the following: 'In the first instance it is highly important that you have personal self-awareness. If you do not understand yourself then you cannot begin to understand others. When I became an assistant headteacher, I remember being told by my mentor that being a leader was about other people – empowering them. That you were no longer the doer. This is very sage advice. As a teacher and a leader I would therefore argue that you must be able to manage your own emotions first and foremost. If you are having a bad day or something is bad in your personal life, you cannot convey this with mood swings, shooting from the hip or being rude toward others. If you are panicked, it is best not to show this to everyone. If you are the headteacher then the outward projection of your mood will impact and reflect on everyone. I also think that it is incredibly important to understand others and to see things from other people's perspectives.' Strickland articulates well how the way in which you come across to your staff is paramount, as is understanding other people's perspectives. Always try to put yourself in their shoes.

The following case study has been provided by Scott Wellington, an assistant headteacher from Gloucester. He discusses how he came to realise the important role that emotional intelligence plays across all aspects of school life. Scott discusses how each person behaves as a teacher and a leader and offers some great insights.

Scott Wellington, assistant headteacher in Gloucester

In my opinion, educators work in an environment that has the potential to make you want to smile, laugh and celebrate successes, yet also cry and want to quit, all in the same day (and that's just by playtime!). Leaders, especially, have to work alongside a wealth of different audiences throughout the course of a week, e.g. children, parents, colleagues and governors. This makes for quite a repertoire of required skills, both interpersonal and also intrapersonal. Emotionally supporting over 30 children in a classroom, offering a listening shoulder to a struggling colleague, taking the brunt of a parent's verbal rampage or providing an emotional sales pitch to a team of governors – it all comes as part of the role. But when I begin thinking about the successes, and failures, of leaders I've seen over the years, there's such a correlation between emotional intelligence and their success rate and the outcomes for the school.

For some leaders and teachers, conflict resolution and overcoming difficulties can be a daily task, dealing with challenging behaviours (not just from children) and being attuned enough to their own emotions and the emotions of all those around in order to deal with situations before they fully arise. This can be the difference between a team thriving and a team crumbling underneath the leader's feet. I truly believe that relationships are key to school success and, in order to build these positive relationships, I believe there are sets of skills, both innate and acquired, that leaders must utilise well, and this will trickle down in every level of the building. To be in a school community full of emotionally intelligent humans who are self-aware, aware of others, share values and motivate one another has to be good for business. Below are some examples of emotional intelligence that have resonated with me over time.

My first real engagement with the leadership at my soon-to-be new school at the time was with the deputy headteacher. I was on my main placement in my second year of my Bachelor of Education course and I had just been told those words that no student wants to hear from their university link tutor: 'You are going to fail this placement!' Was it because I couldn't teach? No. Was it because they felt I wasn't suited to the role? No. Was it because I hadn't seen the point in filling in huge amounts of paperwork along the way, which I was supposed to have done? Definitely.

In the moments after hearing those words, my brain was full of reflective questions: 'How did I let it come to this?', 'How could I have been so stupid?', 'What will Mum think?' and 'Do fast-food restaurants get Ofsted-type visits?' The deputy headteacher heard of the situation and took me for a chat. She listened to my reasoning, giving me an understanding nod every now and then, and then gave me an empowering speech about my next steps. She said, 'No one's perfect.'

After this meeting with the deputy head, in which she said she would smooth it all over with the link tutor, I was given 24 hours to get my paperwork in order. The link tutor was going to come back the next day to see me again. The deputy headteacher sent me home with a list of things I needed to get done and a very honest and inspiring message about her own thoughts on the matter. She had saved my backside.

The empathy that this leader had showed towards me had potentially just saved my career, or at least saved me from another year's worth of university fees. When talking to her about it afterwards, she explained that she could see that I had built great relationships with the children, founded in mutual respect, shown an understanding of ways to help children reach their potential and proved I had the potential to be a sound teacher, and that she believed I could be trusted to learn from that day's events. A year and a half later, that school employed me. Two years afterwards, I was a middle leader there. Four years after that, I got my first assistant headship post. It was safe to say that having this deputy head as a mentor in my early career had helped influence the direction in which my career was going to go and impacted on the way I would see others.

In my time in the teaching profession, emotional intelligence has not been something I've spent too much time reflecting upon. If you asked me ten years ago what I considered to be 'emotional intelligence within the school', I would have probably thought about the crazy, knee-jerk reactions that people in my school and others have had during heat-of-the-moment situations; the inability to see beyond your own pride when dealing with a difficult parent or member of staff (who it turns out had a good point); or the very abrupt way in which some colleagues spoke to others. I originally thought these were just personality quirks of people who probably shouldn't be leaders. However, looking back, I can now see how these situations have often been dictated by people's emotional intelligence (or lack thereof).

In the earliest part of my career, I didn't put much thought into the types of leaders I was surrounded by. But it was soon quite clear that there were leaders who people were drawn to in times of need, and those that they actively avoided. Over time, I had come across plenty of leaders; I always knew which ones I wanted to be like. In terms of career goals, it somehow happened that I realised I wanted to offer that open door where people knew they could come and talk to me; I wanted to be trusted by all of those in the team around me.

One of the first opportunities I got in the profession to be in a role where I was being trusted with extra responsibility was when I was elected as a union representative. The key here was the 'being elected' part. Was this the first time that the team around me was showing me that I was trusted? Did they consider me a listening ear who they could come to in their time of need? Who knows! I've since found out that no one else wanted to do it, but it was still an honour to have that responsibility. My first opportunity to lead an area of education within the team was as ICT coordinator. A passion for technology and an enthusiastic drive for developing computing in the school meant that people listened to me, were motivated by me and followed my lead.

However, over time, I found myself struggling. Not with the workload, not with enthusing the staff to follow my lead, but with everything else that somehow came with the role and that 'open-door' policy I had created for myself. Being greeted at the door in the morning by four teachers and the office staff telling me, 'The server is down' or 'The Key Stage 1 printer needs its waste toner box replacing!' wasn't what I had been sold when I agreed to lead our ICT education forward. It was only when I spent some time reflecting with another new leader at the school that I realised that, by opening myself to everyone, I had left myself vulnerable to some very overpowering needs of others and some problems that I couldn't always help solve. Recognising my own flaw here and how it had happened meant I was able to set myself personal targets of delegating and sometimes just saying 'no'.

During my middle leader qualification, I was fortunate enough to spend some time with experienced coaches from varied education settings, who helped me to reflect on my own practice but also to reflect on my personal qualities such as elements of my emotional intelligence. We were able to unpick areas of strength and areas for development, while also exploring examples of where these have impacted on my practice. We also then spent time looking at who I thought offered a good example of these elements and who I would avoid recommending.

When exploring self-awareness and self-development, I was instantly drawn to the example of a lead I worked under in my early career. She was, bless her, one of the most volatile and explosive characters one moment, and the kindest and most caring in the next. She was experienced and I was in the situation where I needed to come to her for support quite a lot, but I was petrified of what mood she was going to be in. Many described it as 'just the way she is', but any difficult situations for her always exploded into end-of-the-world scenarios, and we found that staff tiptoed around her as they didn't know what was going to come next. She was almost completely unaware that her reactions caused fright in other staff and she certainly didn't see the path of chaos that she left behind, but she was a vital member of the team and we needed her in the school at that time. When she left, her experience and teaching ability was a great loss, but the negative emotions and how challenges were then perceived by the team changed drastically.

Emotional intelligence from a leader can make or break a team. I've seen it happen. In a school where subject 'teams' were put together to help share the workload, those teams with a leader who had a clear set of values that they maintained while listening to the team they were working with and motivating themselves and others through great communication have, in my experience, had far better outcomes. Whereas those leaders who were not as emotionally intelligent could not give consistency, lacked coherence, became erratic in choices or lost trust from their team by placing accountability in all the wrong places. I've found that they have often needed to lead by fear or have simply not led at all.

Think about *that* moment: a phone call comes through for the headteacher, around midday, about a certain visit from a certain team the next day. Of course, a little panic ripples through the senior leadership team as they are told the proceedings for the coming day(s), but consider how they can then react to this. I have come across it played in two different manners. Below are some of the phrases I remember from the first (Team A) and the second (Team B) time it happened. The senior leadership team calls all the teaching staff into the staffroom at the end of the day…

Team A: 'We are being Ofstedded.' 'They have been circling the area recently and we know what they've pulled other schools apart for.' 'Now's the time when we find out whether what we have been doing is right or not.' 'If you've not marked your books by the policy, get it done!'

Team B: 'We're getting some visitors tomorrow of the rather professional sort.' 'We get to showcase all the amazing things we have done as a school.' 'We [the leadership team] get to explore areas we can develop in the school.' 'Don't stick around long tonight, get some sleep, see your family, anything you do now won't make any real difference to tomorrow. You're better off being fresh tomorrow.' 'Let's be proud of what we have done as a school and use this as an opportunity to show how amazing we are.'

Don't the attitude and voice of Team A just ring bells of that person who isn't confident in themselves or in the team around them or perhaps someone that doesn't know how to communicate well or is unable to hold themselves accountable and calm through self-regulation? Sometimes, in moments of challenge, or even utter carnage, we need to have self-control and manage our own emotions, understanding the impact our responses can have on others. Our choice of language, our level of calm, our body language and our choices in the way we express things all matter. Team B trusts their staff. They are ready to take responsibility for the choices they've made over their time leading and they are self-motivated and know how to motivate their staff. What a difference!

As honesty and integrity go, leaders need to know when to put their hands up and be accountable for their actions. I re-quote my old rear-end-saving deputy head: 'No one's perfect.' Our school improvement partner suggested our leadership team take up keeping a journal, and it is something I have found really useful. Recently, I reflected on some heated events that included a time when a parent was not managed best by myself, because I had not taken the time to put thought into the situation. I had been pulled into a meeting with a parent I hadn't met before, who was incredibly irate about the way in which a teacher had apparently spoken to him. He was threatening to go to the press and not return his child to school until that teacher was gone! Without taking in the emotional state of the situation, and without taking a moment to think about the emotions driving his rant, I simply told the gentleman what the complaints procedure in the school was and that I was already made aware that he had approached the teacher in a rather threatening manner. This didn't help him at all! But my colleague who is also on the senior leadership team, who knew the situation a little better, came in and instantly turned the situation around. She listened. She nodded. She then talked about the recent positives with the relationship he had with the school and, like magic, he started to calm. He began to backtrack and, because of her empathetic nature and calm emotional control, she managed to draw out the underlying issues he had: nothing to do with the teacher at all!

I know I handled the situation wrong. But I was brave enough to reflect on this afterwards and talk to the helpful colleague who had de-escalated the situation. I know I need to continue to develop, and having a supportive team around me helps me do this. The integrity and honesty of our team is vital and we continue to grow together because of it. Conflict management and communication are skills that definitely improve over time. We, as a senior leadership team, have more recently been trying to nurture the relationships we have with parents by providing better communication and building stronger bonds with clearer shared visions to ensure that all parents feel actively involved in our school community. We are benefiting from this.

My experience of coaching staff, alongside taking a prominent role in behaviour management within the school, has made me smile on occasion at the similarities in restorative conversations that we have with the children and those that we have with other colleagues. 'Why did you choose to do it this way?' or 'How did that make you (or them) feel?' Of course, reflection is a vital skill here. It is something we have really tried to get our children to learn how to do, and how to do well. It impacts on their world so much. Being able to reflect on their own emotions and the emotions of others can enable children to express themselves, resolve conflicts themselves, hold themselves accountable and communicate better – all things I would want to be able to do well and the things that make life easier if leaders know how to do well. Small reflections and changes can make a big difference: a school-wide ban on Sunday night emailing or my own personal no-later-than-8pm education Twitter scrolling can impact massively on wellbeing.

In recent years, we have gained a new headteacher. Although she wouldn't necessarily label herself an emotionally intelligent person, she is. It has been really impressive watching the whole school community develop and thrive together. The first thing she did was rebuild a shared vision with all stakeholders during INSET. Interestingly, she already had an idea of where she wanted this to go, cleverly listened to people's thoughts and very effectively brought all teams closer together through influenced collaboration. This listening task was a great opportunity for her to show empathy, gather the current politics and emotions of the school and give a level of optimism for the coming days. With her very strong values and clear vision, she has led the way from the front line by regularly teaching in each year group and looks for many opportunities for staff professional development in a low-threat environment. She sits down for coffee with the staff, joking about the antics from the weekend. She puts the children first in absolutely everything she does, ensuring that parents, governors and all of the staff feel incredibly valued along the way. She cares. She really cares. And this doesn't go unnoticed. She smiles and stays consistent; the staff do the same. When the staff smile and remain consistent, the children benefit from this and this impacts on their day-to-day learning. It has been beautiful watching the school community at every level grow together, striving for the best, motivated by the leaders.

I've been very fortunate to work alongside innovative and enthusiastic teams of people who have motivated me to grow. We have achieved some great things and are still continuing on a journey of development. This journey will have its ups and downs like any school's journey, but with emotionally intelligent staff and pupils, being led effectively by emotionally intelligent leaders, we will continue to thrive, creating happy, healthy, lifelong learners.

Scott quite clearly illustrates how important it is to be kind to yourself while you are still learning and, most importantly, to persevere and to not give up too easily.

Thought capsule

Everybody has a vast range of past experiences and so the way each person interprets and reacts to a situation will be very different. Be open to how others may be feeling and monitor how you address situations, both as a teacher and as a leader. Remember that how someone reacts isn't personal; it is very much about their emotion and their interpretation of the situation.

5
Autonomy

It is vital that we encourage and reach out to those who are yet to take their first steps and also those who are pushing themselves out of their comfort zones. This is one of the many reasons why I've wanted to capture words of wisdom from other professionals, in the form of case studies, throughout this book.

Sarah Mullin, deputy headteacher and author of *What They Didn't Teach Me on my PGCE* (2019)

Rather than being enticed by prestigious job titles, lucrative salaries, a private office or a designated car parking space, most teachers and leaders would probably agree that we are driven by a genuine desire to create positive change.

Great teachers and leaders will take others with them on their journey to success, helping them to see light in the darkness and clarity in the confusion. We would not be where we are today if it was not for the guidance, wisdom and support of those who have mentored us, challenged us and given us the opportunities we needed to flourish as leaders in education. As school leaders, we can also create a culture where other staff are motivated, inspired and empowered to be the best they can be. It is our responsibility as leaders to nurture, support and develop future educational leaders by providing a range of opportunities to enable colleagues to reach their potential. As we climb the career ladder, it is important for us to reach out and help those who are yet to take their first steps. We need to encourage colleagues to step out of their comfort zones so that they are able to challenge themselves.

In order to take those first steps and move forward, we need to know that we are supported and, crucially, trusted.

Ritesh Patel, teacher and leader of design and technology at Prendergast Ladywell School

I have developed an understanding of the value of trust within a team and how it has a positive impact on individual and team goals. Ultimately, we have to acknowledge trust is never instantaneous. I have always followed a model where I identify individual strengths as a platform to build this trust. Constructive and encouraging communication helps teachers to grow and flourish, which essentially drives autonomy. Strong leaders are motivators and develop new leaders. I believe a consistent and supportive environment embeds confidence and productivity. And with this in mind, always refer to the bigger picture; our students are benefiting from happy teachers. We must show faith in our teachers. Tell them we believe in them. Praise them. Thank them. The small things really do matter. It can be small to some but a game changer for others. The beauty of living in such a diverse world has made us learn and appreciate unique individuality. Teachers are not just teachers. A teacher is a human being with emotions that have to respected and trusted.

Trust

I'm sure many of you would agree that micro-managing to the nth degree just does not work and can drive good teachers away. If you think about our emotional wellbeing, at the heart of it is trust. Trust in personal relationships, as well as trust between colleagues, is a huge factor. Once trust is lost, it can take a long while to restore and, in some cases, it can be lost indefinitely. So many leaders have broken this trust because they have proven themselves to be inconsistent in their approach, leading with a dictatorship-style attitude and constantly pushing others down to raise themselves higher. I am certain many of you reading this book can picture a manager or a leader that you have worked with, or known, that fits into these categories quite well. I'm also sure that you will agree that none of these attributes should be present within an individual that works alongside teachers and children. Unfortunately, it is still the case that some leaders do seemingly 'get away' with treating others badly, 'fooling' the governors and 'playing the part' in the eyes of more senior executive colleagues.

In the following case study, submitted by a former multi-trust teacher from Suffolk, they discuss the benefits of working for an emotionally intelligent headteacher that truly trusts their staff. They compare the crucial differences between a headteacher that is invested in their staff and those that are just paying lip service in order to achieve results.

Anonymous teacher

I have worked under several different headteachers in my career. Each one has had their own strengths and weaknesses and has helped to shape my practice as a teacher.

There has been a lot of talk on 'EduTwitter' in recent months about emotional intelligence and the role of the headteacher. I will be discussing emotional intelligence and how it can affect the relationship and trust between headteachers and their staff.

From my experience of working in a multi-academy trust, the 'managers' at the top pride themselves on knowing the names of every individual but could not tell you anything directly personal about these individuals. When a conversation is held, it becomes very singular as there is no genuine interest in what the individual is talking about. The other person is already preoccupied with their next conversation or their next area of interest. This is in contrast to a teacher who can tell you the name of each child in their class and many more around the school. This teacher is able to have meaningful conversations with them based on talking to the team to get to know them and what interests them.

Brené Brown talks about empathy and sympathy in her TED Talk, 'The power of vulnerability'. I believe vulnerability generates the pathway to trust.

Empathy is an important ingredient for building a relationship with your co-workers and the children you teach. How many times have you had one of those light bulb moments with a child when you share a common experience and from that moment there is a new understanding and a genuine connection? When, as teachers, we make this connection with a pupil or colleague, then the element of trust and relatability improves immensely. Sympathy is effective in making an initial connection but it doesn't make for a long-term one. Which would you prefer from your headteacher? Knowing that they are willing to share and make a connection by showing understanding via personal experience or just getting a minimal response that you could fit on the back of a postage stamp?

It is usually easy to tell when a smile is genuine and when it is just a reactionary trigger to pleasantries. A leader with emotional intelligence is able to read the emotions of their employees and able to nurture them in order to benefit the team. This was unfortunately not the case at my last school. I watched employees quietly ushered into the head's office and it normally resulted in one outcome: somebody walking out, clearly distressed and in a very negative state of mind, the main cause of this being the lack of compassion from the leader and their inability to use empathy to forge a connection.

If a teacher walks into the headteacher's office, the headteacher should sit down with them and offer support and demonstrate praise where due, which instantly makes them feel better. They should be solution-focused, while remaining compassionate. When a leader adopts this approach, the teacher called in to be offered support feels valued and appreciated. Recognising this basic human need – to be supported and understood – goes a long way. People with high emotional intelligence are socially perceptive at recognising and understanding the feelings and emotions in their team (Steiner, 1972) and induce positive emotions and attitudes in others (Bono and Ilies, 2006).

When learning walks take place under this kind of difficult leader, there can be a constant feeling of self-doubt in your ability to teach. Learning walks can be viewed as a positive and enriching experience but they can also lead to a lack of confidence and elevate negative feelings. Of course, if you don't feel threatened and trust your leadership team, learning walks wouldn't affect you as much. But consider that there is no trust and your leadership team can be inconsistent with the way they treat you – where does that leave you? Completely and utterly fearful of such learning walks.

In a profession that has an awfully low level of retention, we need to do something to buck the trend. We need to examine the internal workings of each school – the teachers, senior leadership team and governors – and we need to make sure that everyone connected with schools is supportive, thoughtful and trustworthy in their approach. Would we still be losing teachers if their headteachers were supporting them? Would they still be leaving if, when they went to their headteachers with a problem, they felt they were being listened to? I think not. Leaders set the tone for the culture of their school.

Trust is a huge stakeholder within the dynamics of a team. If trust is to be valued and utilised on a day-to-day basis then it needs to be underpinned by the leadership team. If any of their behaviour, or way of exerting their leadership onto others, does not demonstrate that they trust their staff, then it becomes just another buzzword with absolutely no meaning.

Confidentiality

Trust is built when the leader knows their true role. They understand that they cannot blur the lines between what should be confidential information and what should be openly discussed. Staff are more likely to come with problems to discuss and solve if they know that the discussion will remain private. If there is any inkling about the leadership team leaking information, or discussing with others unnecessarily, then key discussions that should take place will not, and this in turn can cause the 'whispering in the corridor' effect.

This effect is seen when, instead of problems being professionally discussed and solved, members of staff take it upon themselves to try to solve the problem during the school day through the medium of offloading and quick discussions that aim to be supportive, but in actual fact are not. The problem is this: what started out as a small issue spirals out of control and becomes a negative situation. Emotions become heightened and gossip and the 'what ifs?' become fraught with tension, when really this whole situation could have been avoided completely. When a leader shows complete trust and integrity, these situations tend not to occur, and if they do, they are dealt with quickly in a proactive, positive manner.

For a member of teaching staff to trust a leader, they need to know that they are willing to give consistent and honest support. Heidi Collier-Brown, a Year 6 teacher I have worked alongside, says: 'During the lead-up to SATs, a member of my team was struggling with mental health problems without them even realising. I had to consider how to approach this, share my concern about their health with them and support them through such a tough time in the academic year.'

Dr Andrew Curran (2021) has found that 'Twenty-five years of neurobiological research tells us that children learn best when they feel loved.' This is very much the same for adults, but the love is expressed in the form of appreciation and trust – knowing that you can express how you feel, ask questions and risk-take without the worry of having a black mark against your name for doing so. This is by no means encouraging question after question. Instead, it is very much about the idea that, at times, questions need to be asked to gain clarity, fully understand a situation or process why someone has behaved in a certain way.

Dr Curran goes on as follows: 'We must never lose sight of the human being in front of us. In the same way that a good doctor looks beyond the symptoms and the illness to the well person that lies beneath, a good teacher will look beyond behaviours and academic outcomes to a child who wants to learn and is capable of learning. One who is so much more than their behaviours or academic results.'

So, what do I mean by complete trust?

Personally, I believe that if a person shows trust in all capacities it means that every single action, word and presence radiates trust. Here is some sage advice from James Hilton (2018, pg. 59) on how to put this into practice:

'**Always keep confidences where you can** – However don't promise confidentiality if you are unsure whether you should keep the information from other people, e.g. performance or ethical issues.

Give credit where credit is due – Acknowledge the contributions of others. Be an advocate for other people.

Never talk about other people behind their backs, unless you have something positive to say – If you do, others will assume you are doing the same to them. Again "what goes around…"

Make sure your messages are consistent – Don't say different things to different people in an effort to please.

If you are asked a question, then give a complete and direct answer – So no smoke and mirrors. If you don't have the answer, don't try to bluff it. If I am put on the spot, which happens when you are teaching, I always say "I will get back to you" and by the close of day I will have the situation that has been brought to me, resolved.'

While keeping all of these elements in mind, it is important that you demonstrate hope and trust while not coming across as naive. I believe it is important to be a 'tsunami of optimism' but you need to remain realistic and not walk around with your head in the clouds, so to speak. You need to keep your feet on the ground and your wits about you.

Perception

I am very much a realist; however, I also have a huge amount of positive energy because it is needed to get you through each school day! When I find myself thinking too much about a situation, I remind myself that I've done what I said I would do, and have remained consistent and true to my word. That is sometimes all you can do – how others choose to perceive your actions is their responsibility. It is an unfortunate truth that people who 'focus in' on the negative will always find it, the same as when you 'focus in' on the positive: if you are looking for it, you are likely to be greeted with it. It is all about perspective and how you manifest each situation.

The following is a question I've considered quite often lately. I think it is important that you ask yourself this question:

Am I observing the situation accurately or am I projecting how I feel onto what is actually happening?

I think we naturally project past traumas onto situations and words that are said in the present. The situation and words can often conjure up memories, so you naturally relive the hurt because it is stored in your hippocampus and amygdala. The amygdala stores the memory and the hippocampus sequences and filters the memory of events. With this in mind, it is important that leaders choose their words and actions as carefully as they can. Leaders are not responsible for past hurts and worries, but it is their responsibility to ensure that each situation that is dealt with, no matter how difficult, makes each person in the room feel valued, respected and listened to.

Trusting the emotions of the person whom you go to for support is vital, but we must remember that each one of us is a human being. The person supporting you has their own challenges, too.

Ian Armstrong, deputy headteacher at Ivy School House

I read a book on leadership a few years back (*Brave Heads* by Dave Harris, 2013) and it said that a good leader was someone who portrayed a constant emotional state, regardless of how they actually felt on the inside. From my years working in mainstream school, I agreed with this statement and felt like a leader should be a calm, robotic-like figure who had all the answers. However, when I moved into leadership, perhaps because I worked in an SEMH school where staff were dealing with challenging behaviours and safeguarding issues, my own leadership style was very different from this. While sometimes there is a need for the leader to remain calm and 'have all the answers', I believe it is also important to show empathy and be self-aware. It is OK to be criticised and apologise if you make the wrong decision, as long as you learn from your mistakes and become a better leader as a result of it.

Of course, we can't promise to be calm at all times, but we can make sure that we are as calm as possible at the outset of any interaction. As a leader, this is important to do as it keeps others calm around you. Think of the analogy of the swan who appears graceful, elegant and unruffled on the surface of the lake, but is paddling like crazy underneath! Having said this, when you need to show your emotion in a direct, clear-cut fashion, it *is* healthy for others to see this, as they can ascertain that, as well as being calm and in control, you are also very passionate about what you stand for.

Admitting errors

I think it is important to point out that of course we all make mistakes – to err is human – but they should be as few as possible. Holding your hands up and saying, 'I was wrong' is so important; if you do not admit to your errors, your staff will not trust your words.

I think we mostly know this to be true when we reflect upon the Covid-19 pandemic and how some political leaders have handled the situation. If you dodge a question, or divert attention with nonsensical facts and figures, your audience will see straight through you. Most will agree that, when it comes to politicians, we would rather they were honest: if they don't know the answer to a question, they should say as much, not just smile, cover it up and pretend all is well. The same applies to teachers and leaders in schools.

Adam Newman, curriculum leader at Farmilo Primary School

In a sports context, the half-time team talk is a good example of where I have observed high levels of emotional intelligence – and the very opposite. In elite sports settings, the stakes are always high and the leader has very little time to 'press reset' on some behaviours, feelings and thoughts. Tony Smith, one of the most successful Super League coaches, is a master of emotionally intelligent communication. While we may have the preconception that half-time communication is one-way, from coach to player (often in a ranting style), Tony would always calmly ask, 'What just happened?', 'Why?', followed with 'How are we going to handle this?'. By meeting the players where they are, he would and could shape his message effectively.

I often think of high-quality sports coaching when I think of emotional intelligence. It requires the ability to quickly read the whole situation and chip in with praise at those peak times to accelerate performance and prevent someone from falling below the line. It requires being able to juggle all of the players' emotions in one fell swoop, and still make those marginal gains.

During Day 11 of the 2021 Australian Open at Melbourne Park, Serena Williams was defeated in the women's singles semi-final against Naomi Osaka of Japan. Following the defeat, Williams made the following comment: 'The difference today was errors… I made too many mistakes, easy mistakes, not like I was on the run or anything. It was just a big error day for me today.' (Zetlin, 2021)

Notice that Serena didn't blame the judges, the court surface or her injuries for her failure. She owned the failure completely. This is a brave and resilient move to acknowledge and accept her errors. It was a big error day for her, but tomorrow would be another new day!

Being self-aware and knowing where you have made an error is hugely advantageous to performance. For teachers, knowing that you are trusted to make errors is the first step to intelligent risk-taking.

Flexibility

Teachers who are trusted to work in a way that suits them often produce excellent results. In his recent work, Daniel H Pink writes that 'on the edges of the economy – slowly, but inexorably – old-fashioned ideas of management are giving way to a new-fangled emphasis on self-direction. That's why, a little past noon on a rainy Friday in Charlottesville, only a third of CEO Jeff Gunther's employees have shown up for work. But Gunther – entrepreneur, manager, capitalist – is neither worried nor annoyed. In fact, he's as calm and focused as a monk. Or maybe that's because he knows his crew isn't shirking. They're working – just on their own terms.' (Pink, 2009, pg. 85)

Gunther's staff were still working but self-directing and achieving great things because of this. This sense of autonomy allows each person to feel trusted, respected and safe.

Sam Strickland summarises this perfectly: 'It's important to say that lines of communication do need to be kept open, to ensure that staff don't fall into the waves of inertia, because they've become isolated with their own regime. Effective communication and autonomy is what keeps the ship afloat and understanding your staff and the way they choose to work keeps that ship on track; therefore the school culture thrives.' (Strickland, 2020, pg. 80)

Someone who is already conscientious and places pressure on themselves to do a good job doesn't need to be micro-managed or directed, because they are already completely self-motivated. Once you destroy someone's autonomy and take away their independence, the person's confidence will waiver and this takes a long while to recover. It takes an emotionally intelligent mind to keep that confidence burning bright.

Pink states that, 'A sense of autonomy has a powerful effect on individuals' performance and attitude. According to a cluster of recent behavioral science studies, autonomous motivation promotes greater conceptual understanding, better grades, enhanced persistence at school and in sporting activities, higher productivity, less burnout and greater levels of psychological wellbeing. Those effects carry over to the workplace.' (Pink, 2009, pg. 91)

It's so true, isn't it? The more you are trusted, the better the job you will do.

Workload

As mentioned previously in Chapter 4, quite often it isn't the workload that is the issue; it is the workload combined with a toxic environment that pushes educators to the edge.

In the following case study, Sam Strickland discusses how to manage workload expectations. Whether you find yourself in a school full of trust or a school full of toxic compliance, managing your workload effectively is one small step towards taking charge of your environment. The advice is simple: control the controllable; work with what you have.

Sam Strickland, author and principal of Duston School

There are many case study examples that I could give where emotional intelligence has played a part in positively dealing with a member of staff or a situation, all the way to a positive resolution. However, I wanted to share a few examples of pre-emptive, proactive approaches that you can take. These approaches are designed to deal with staff workload, the aim being to help mitigate against future issues.

In creating a series of measures or a workload charter to support staff, you are clearly showing to people that you have emotional intelligence. A key to being a good senior leader in a school is to never lose sight of what it is to be a class-based teacher. To do so shows that you are out of touch with the daily routine of being a teacher. We should never forget that teaching is hard. Teachers have to perform, day in and day out, for four to six hours a day. They have to make hundreds of split-second decisions every day. They have to be experts in their field. Their subject knowledge has to be exemplary. They have to deal with behaviour – be it good, bad or indifferent. They also have to mark, plan, devise curriculums, respond to parents and undertake any other tasks as deemed fit by the head. It is not a 9.00 am to 3.00 pm role. Far from.

So, how can we pre-emptively help staff manage their workload? I want to share four pre-emptive approaches.

Firstly, consider carefully how you structure your meeting schedule. I would argue that the most important meeting slot, over and above any other, is time for departments or teams to meet and discuss the curriculum and subject knowledge. I challenge whether senior teams really need to be so directional with middle leaders that pre-populated meeting agendas are issued. My feeling is that you should train your middle leaders to fully understand what the curriculum is and then give them the free licence, i.e. time with their team, to work on this. If you give time in this manner then staff will be able to map and plan their curriculum; they will have time to upskill and enhance their subject knowledge; they will have the time to truly consider the enacted curriculum; and they will have the time to co-plan. The benefits, if you strike this balance correctly, can be exponential. Staff will grow in confidence, they will appreciate the devolved use of time and, more importantly, the enacted curriculum will strengthen, strengthen and strengthen. Critically, staff will, over time, cease to feel over-worked and over-burdened. With the same token, you could also carefully consider how you utilise your five training days of the year and whether you offer faculty away-days.

Secondly, I would carefully consider the institutional approach to emails. Emails can be a real burden for staff. They can cause staff extreme stress and create a lot of disgruntlement. I would actually argue that most emails are tosh and if an email is much more than four lines long, it warrants a meeting. Personally, I do not feel we should be emailing each other about work-related matters at weekends and holidays. We should respect that we are not at work and that people need a break. If you have layered your meeting schedule carefully, as outlined in the first point, then you are affording people the time and air space to engage in face-to-face dialogue.

Thirdly, I think we should carefully consider how we approach data. Do we need six data captures a year? I would argue that two or three data drops per academic year is sufficient. This can then be linked to the overall assessment model within your school. Lots of self- or peer-marked low-stakes retrieval practice quizzes have a far greater impact on a pupil's long-term schemas than endless 'weigh the pig'-style high-stakes tests. This, in turn, significantly reduces the amount of marking that staff have to undertake and, again, positively impacts on workload.

Finally, the approach a school takes to behaviour is also key. Are things left solely to the teacher? Is the approach one of creating hero teachers, while letting the rest sink? I would personally advocate a centralised approach to student care and behaviour, with senior staff and senior leaders taking the lead on this. In centralising everything and ensuring that support comes from above, staff are able to consider and concentrate on teaching and not just dealing with behaviour on repeat. Again, this will save people a lot of time, they will feel supported and, more importantly, the enacted curriculum benefits.

Thought capsule

Giving and receiving trust is crucial when you want to develop and create a strong school culture. Trust is built upon a number of consistent interactions, when words match actions and when each person in the school building feels trusted to risk-take and achieve their potential.

6
Leadership

Dr Jill Berry suggests that being a good leader is 'about self-awareness, awareness of others and the ability to be able to empathise and see issues from others' perspectives'. Jill subsequently goes on to use three words to define emotional intelligence: 'sensitivity, humanity and understanding' (2019).

I think there can be a sense that a leader is 'soft' in their approach if they encompass the qualities that Dr Berry describes, but the reality is that leaders who embrace these traits are far more effective because they implicitly understand the emotions that are being filtered behind the scenes and how they are played out in often difficult situations. Emotional intelligence and leadership should be intrinsically linked and the emotionally intelligent professional must never be seen as a weak link or a 'soft touch'.

Misconceptions

At the heart of a school environment should be trust, autonomy, happiness, humour and a leader that understands and values their colleagues. As Cowley states, 'team spirit, standing by and standing up for colleagues, a positive culture and leaders who want to make this work provide the best foundations for a school where the wellbeing of the staff and children is truly valued.' (Cowley, 2019, pg. 61)

Protecting the wellbeing of staff is fundamental and there have been many misconceptions about teaching that have been circulating for years. Sam Strickland sets out some common misconceptions about teaching in the chapter 'Protecting staff' in his book *Education Exposed* (2020).

1. 'Teaching should hurt.

2. Teachers need to be in at 7am and should not leave until at least 6pm.

3. Teachers need to regulate their own workload and any attempt to do so by SLT is to stifle free choice.

4. Planning is a skill that should be mastered in isolation.

5. Being busy means you are effective.

6. Lots of emails mean a good job is being performed and everyone understands.'

(Strickland, 2020, pg. 75)

These are misconceptions and will be identified as such if the school has a strong leadership team who demonstrate a collective and shared strong sense of values. To drive a high-functioning workforce and facilitate high performance, a leadership team should know what empathy is and how each member of their team differs, and understand everyone's way of working and processing daily tasks and new information. 'We as educational professionals aren't trained to diagnose mental health issues, but we can perhaps identify situations where pressure, stress and deadlines can impact upon our colleagues. […] Some of our colleagues are more vulnerable than others. This is not something to be judgemental about; it requires compassion, understanding and humanity.' (Cowley, 2019, pg. 60)

Of course we have a job to do, but however we go about achieving results there should be humanity at all times. I feel strongly about this. One of the main reasons I chose to move on from my last school was because the academy made a staff member reapply for her job while she was undergoing treatment for cancer. How could they do that to another person, to a fellow human being? Why and how was that ever appropriate? No thought, care or consideration was demonstrated.

Unreasonable behaviour

As a teacher and leader, I've never been one to accept unreasonable behaviour; what I have done, over the years, is remembered that specific behaviour and made the decision that I would never repeat that behaviour when I became a leader. I've realised that my values are very strong and so when someone treats me and others badly, it makes me think about what that person is trying to achieve by putting others down or trying to exclude them from situations. Most often it could be that the person in question feels insecure and is trying to bring you down a notch or two. It can also boil down to professional jealousy. It is important to remember that jealousy comes from insecurity in a person, so it is always better to work with the root cause as much as you can.

Support that person; look beyond their surface reactions and behaviour.

Leadership v management v human nature – the challenge

'We forget sometimes that "management" does not emanate from nature. It's not like a tree or a river. It's like a television or a bicycle. It's something that humans invented.' (Pink, 2009, pg. 88)

Management can be looked upon as something that is just a driver of results, no matter how you get there. The main factor of management is control. Within leadership, you can reduce that control by letting the team drive you and working together to achieve results. Controlling all scenarios gets you nowhere; it's akin to micro-managing. Of course there still needs to be an element of control with the direction that is taken as a school, but all parties of the leadership team should be stakeholders on the journey, with shared responsibility and shared action.

Human nature and 'cold' management do not run hand in hand. Leadership is a shared, natural progression, as suggested earlier, like 'a tree or a river'; however, management is very much a mechanical, forced process.

The following case study from Michael, a secondary teacher, analyses and presents his own views of how a leadership and management team clearly drive culture, values and ethos throughout a school. This is his personal account of a succession of negative experiences in a recent school.

Michael, classroom teacher in a secondary school

When I was a good few years into teaching, I felt it was the right time for a change. Moving house had led to a back-pain-inducing commute, and the prospect of teaching at the same school for the rest of my career was somewhat bleak. So I applied for a sideways move as teacher of science and was successful. The school and its pupils seemed well-managed and the teachers in the department – like me – were young, enthusiastic and sociable. On the interview day and the training days, I fitted in well. I even met some of the staff over the summer when I went in to do up my new classroom. I was feeling positive about September.

I began my new post at the same time as the new head of department, Joanne. Joanne and I built a strong relationship pretty quickly – probably because we were both new and shared similar attitudes. Unlike the staff in our department, we had a far wider experience of the education system and because of this there were significant aspects of the school management that we struggled with.

The school I came from was by no means perfect (which school is?) but my previous headteacher regularly made a point of saying 'we are in this together' during difficult times, and it was considered uncouth for a school leader to talk down to a teacher. Also, the decision-making process largely involved all stakeholders. Because of this and similar 'taken-for-granted' experiences at my previous school, certain things about my new school made me feel a bit uncomfortable.

Team spirit was not really promoted. Rather, teachers were encouraged to view each other as competition. For example, the school had what they referred to as an 'open-door' policy. In the context of this school, it meant that teachers were permitted to conduct a 'learning walk' on any other teacher in the school. This is fine if the aim is professional development, but the problem was that no notice period was stipulated, no permission was required and, to make it worse, the feedback could be published on the shared area for the whole school to see. In short, if a geography teacher dropped in on an English teacher on Friday Period 5 after a lunchtime fight and the class was out of control, they were free to write exactly this on a spreadsheet where everyone could see it.

It would be disrespectful to fellow teachers to assume that a significant number of us would be that underhanded and vindictive, so not for a second did I believe this to be the case. Rather, I assumed that most teachers probably wouldn't even conduct learning walks – let alone vindictive ones – because of the obvious reason: lack of time. What didn't help, however, was how desperate everyone seemed to be either to impress or to avoid the wrath of some member of SLT – 'Does so and so know you've done that?', 'Has so and so seen that?', 'What if so and so finds out?', 'Run it by so and so' and 'So and so will be well chuffed with that!'. I'd never known such persistent involvement of an SLT in the daily lives of teachers. I figured it was inevitable that some teachers would be terrified enough to make others look bad in order to make themselves look good, and so I became suspicious of the nature of the learning walks.

The totalitarian nature of SLT was as publicly displayed as it was privately discussed. Every morning at 8.35 am, staff were to attend briefing in the staffroom. The SLT running the briefing did not arrive – as if religiously – until 8.40 am. After deliberately making everyone wait five minutes, all ten of them would assemble at the front, one by one, and await silence from their humble, terrified subordinates. The smiling, charismatic headteacher, backed by his unsavoury looking deputy heads, would then begin his pretentiously positive spiel for the day.

Ironically, at the time, emotional intelligence was something of a hot topic in schools. At my previous school it was mentioned as a matter of course in any behaviour management training session and it formed a significant part of the training for middle leaders. It was a shock to me, then, that my new school did not mention it at all! It seemed that the primary motivator was fear, and the carrot was the occasional head-nod from someone very high in the hierarchy. The stick, in the form of micro-management, was used to beat all and relationships were transactional, not personal. What was to ensue during my time there, I believe, was a product of the voluntary forfeiture of emotional intelligence. No doubt some school leaders don't have it, but in this case, I believe it was deliberately ignored, particularly empathy, essentially because bad school leaders believe that doing the best for pupils necessitates the poor treatment of teachers.

Joanne and I could not ascribe to this school's 'non-ethos'.

It wasn't long before it became obvious that Joanne had no power as head of department. If not being allowed to decide which pupils were to do the higher or foundation GCSE paper wasn't bad enough (something SLT interfered with), Joanne wasn't even allowed to choose the colour of the exercise books for Key Stage 3 pupils.

Her line manager, one of the aforementioned deputy heads, Olivia, had, in hindsight, a personality that can only really be described as sociopathic. Olivia would overrule any decision made by Joanne and would berate her loudly and clearly in meetings. 'We do what's best for the kids!' she would shout. The 'enthusiastic' staff I spoke of earlier? They were very friendly with Olivia and would often undermine Joanne. I backed Joanne from the get-go, not only because we became friends, but also because the only thing she was 'guilty' of in my mind was simply doing things differently. It wasn't long before Joanne was regularly being 'learning walked', harassed with emails and called into meetings and I recall reassuring her when she cried on a handful of occasions. This stayed with me for a long time. I mean, seeing your line manager cry at work is one thing, and it's bad enough in itself, but as a young member of staff it put me off going for any promotion for a long time. Only after some serious consideration did I ever apply for a Teaching and Learning Responsibility.

The school didn't tell me that Saturday revision sessions ran frequently over the year. In other words, this was an expectation of staff, and not one I was willing to live up to. So every time a timetable came round where staff were expected to sign their names to commit to a given Saturday, I was looked at with disdain when I didn't. Another deputy head, Steve, was particularly clever with his coercion. He would make statements such as: 'We're not expecting all staff to do *every* Saturday.' In other words, we have to do *some* Saturdays. I didn't do any, and as a result the whole department would receive emails from the head of physics, who would mention my groups as 'key groups' that 'need intervention' and that he's 'disappointed' that the classes won't get a Saturday session so he needs more volunteers. I was constantly being undermined. To make it worse, a couple of colleagues would drop into my lessons with a clipboard, plant themselves at the back and refuse to give me immediate feedback by saying, 'You'll see it once it's published.' Then on the spreadsheet I'd read comments that were either pernickety or inane. Sadly, my initial fear of learning walks was fully justified.

With Joanne being constantly inappropriately challenged, me defending her and also refusing to do Saturday interventions, it became obvious that I was now at the top of the 'hit list'. The head of physics would often publicly question my dedication, backhandedly disguising it as humour. Conversations would stop when either myself or Joanne entered the room and passive-aggressive comments were constantly made. I felt my anxiety and stress mounting, particularly when I found out what Olivia did to people who didn't work on Saturdays: the following year they were teaching in up to 20 different rooms, i.e. not a single lesson in the same classroom – a way to impact any teacher's wellbeing and potentially ruin their career as a result.

Soon enough, it was time for us to do controlled assessments for GCSE. I followed the guidelines to the letter, yet the majority of my pupils got Ds and Es while my less experienced colleagues' classes were getting A*s. It was all very 'hush-hush', but between the pupils and the inability of my colleagues to keep their mouths shut, it became obvious: they were cheating. And I don't mean 'giving-a-bit-too-much-help' cheating, I mean 'mark-scheme-on-the-board' cheating. I kept quiet as everyone pretty much hated me and Joanne by then, so there was no point in rocking the boat further.

I was then approached by Steve to discuss my poor results. He asked me to repeat the assessments after school, which would have taken at least two hours per group. I point-blank told him that the only reason everyone else's results were higher was because they were cheating. He ignored me and said that the pupils had *got* to get As and it was just a matter of repeating the assessments. I told him I wasn't going to stay behind after school to repeat something I did right the first time and they couldn't make me anyway with trade union regulations, etc. He left abruptly, then came back the next day with a threat that would tip my mental health over the edge: he told me that the head had said that they *could* make me because as a school we were under the 1,265 hours of directed time, and 'When writing a reference, the head has to tick a "yes or no" box stating whether he would employ you again. Which one do you think he'd tick?'

From this point on, I had anxiety that probably required medication. I remember chain-smoking in my car at 7.00 am after many a poor night's sleep, thinking and worrying,

'Am I stuck here forever? I can't cope with 20 different rooms! Is my career over? I've just bought a house!' As well as the sleepless nights, the random waking-up times and the loss of appetite, not-so-rational catastrophising thoughts insidiously occupied my mind and refused to leave. Steve got me good. I wanted to see a doctor but my then not-so-enlightened or self-considered self thought that taking stress leave would be a sign of weakness. Oh, how ignorant I was.

After Googling lots of teacher forums and seeing how many teachers had suffered the way I was, I found the number for a whistle-blowing hotline. I figured that the school were out to ruin me so I might as well fight back and tell whoever that their controlled assessments were not so controlled. Unfortunately (or perhaps fortunately), and for various reasons, the union office told me not to – so I didn't.

Thankfully, Joanne repeated the assessments for me, and I just kept my head down and got on with my job. I made an effort with my colleagues, who would continue to undermine me, and I even offered to do extra revision sessions after school to make up for the ones I wasn't doing on a Saturday. I just couldn't handle any more bullying (in hindsight, that's exactly what this was) so I ate humble pie.

I left that school within the academic year, courtesy of a friend who told me about a job at her school and put in a 'good word' for me. I put Joanne as a reference and the head either didn't care or didn't notice.

Unfortunately, there are some schools out there that even the plague would avoid. I believe it's our duty to speak out about them.

Ulterior motives, ethics and values

The definition of an ulterior motive is 'a secret purpose or reason for doing something' (Cambridge Advanced Learner's Dictionary & Thesaurus, 2013).

As I've moved into leadership, I've had to savvy up and realise not everyone says exactly what they mean. You have to unpick the scenarios (at times) to reveal a hidden motive. To be very honest, it makes me uncomfortable to think or analyse others in this way, as I would expect others to say what they mean, as I do. But, unfortunately, not everyone has honest intentions, especially in positions of leadership and influence.

A concrete example has been contributed by an education professional and is a genuine, authentic account of a situation that they were placed in at school following a recent promotion to the wider leadership team.

Darius, a maths teacher within a large team

I successfully applied for a leadership role with whole-school responsibility. Several months after my promotion, there was an internal disciplinary investigation into another maths teacher's behaviours – nothing particularly sinister – but the feeling was that SLT wanted this particular teacher 'out'.

I was approached by the headteacher, outside of the investigation, and the conversation went something like this:

Head: You worked with him in the maths department, you must know what he's like? Perhaps you should put a statement in about what you saw and heard during your time there.

Darius: I haven't worked in the team for a while now though. Of course I know him; he's a good teacher, he's a colleague and a personal friend. I really don't want to get involved. It would break my relationship with him and the whole team.

Head: Well, Darius, you're in the leadership team now. It will be interesting to see where your loyalties lie…

I did not submit a statement as part of the disciplinary process and instead took the opportunity to leave the school at the end of the academic year.

During the course of my research for this book, I spoke to an assistant headteacher (anonymised as Hannah at their request) who was told by their head to investigate a teacher who had allegedly told a pupil to 'f**k off'. Now, I think we would all struggle to imagine any professional anywhere ever saying something like that to a young person, but the head was adamant that an investigation should take place. Allegedly, the pupil had reported the comment to the head, and the AHT now had to discuss the allegation with the teacher. The AHT was told in no uncertain terms (by the head) that she should talk to the teacher, explain the allegation and tell him that a formal disciplinary investigation would be undertaken, and that this could result in dismissal. The head went on to add that if, however, the teacher wished to tender their resignation at this point, then of course it would be accepted, and the allegation would be dropped.

What a position the AHT was in at this point. Would she carry out the instructions of the headteacher, instructions that she disagreed with, and potentially ruin a fellow professional's career? Would she challenge her line manager and headteacher and refuse? Would she whistle-blow? What would the consequences of that be? The AHT had a 'conversation' with the teacher, who subsequently left the meeting citing that they felt unwell (understandably so) and was never seen at school again. Their resignation followed within days – as did the resignation of the AHT, who moved on after finding that the culture of the school and the values driven by the head did not align with her own moral compass.

McClelland's Needs Theory

David McClelland, a psychologist working in the 1950s to 1990s, developed a model that describes how four different motivations can drive managerial behaviour. The four needs that the model describes are: achievement, affiliation, power and avoidance. It is the fourth need, avoidance, that applies when we think about ulterior motives.

Skills
and
knowledge

Visible

Invisible

Opinions and values

Qualities and driving factors

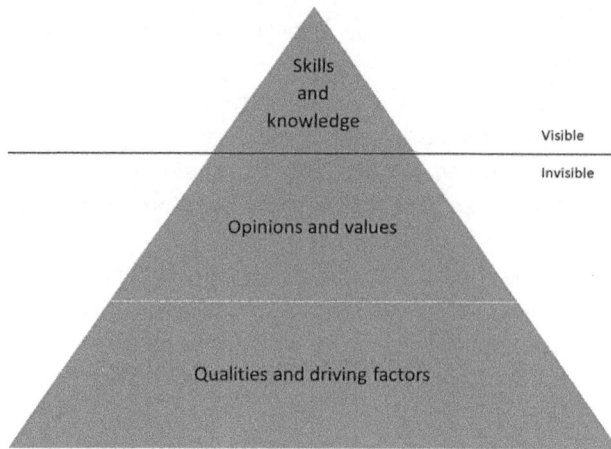

Figure 2: McClelland's iceberg model, adapted from Mulder (2015)

People avoid situations that make them feel uncomfortable. The need for avoidance can account for people having or demonstrating ulterior motives. These ulterior motive requests cover up the fact that the individual feels uncomfortable. The need for avoidance, researched by David McClelland, occurs when people have experienced rejection, failure or even a fear of success. By avoiding situations that trigger these emotions, it means they ultimately feel safe.

McClelland's iceberg model looks at a person's visible behaviour, knowledge and skills and the underlying unexpressed and subconscious deeper layers.

In general, a person's knowledge, skills and behaviour can be found above the waterline of the iceberg. The central element is what they do. Below the waterline we find 'think' and 'want', which focus on abstract terms such as standards, values and beliefs, self-esteem, characteristics, personality and motives. These four invisible layers could reinforce one another as motives. However, they may also block the visible behaviour of the person in question (Mulder, 2015).

McClelland's iceberg model applies to each of us. What we can view at surface level in one another is really a tiny snapshot of the overall person.

I've made reference to intuition several times already throughout this book, but I have another question about it: if intuition is strong and valid, then how is it that a person's intuition does not always spot ulterior motives in other people? Is it because you wouldn't expect others to be thinking in this way and a natural reaction is to hope that they are being honest with their words and actions? Or is it because you would only spot this if you yourself possess this tendency to act with ulterior motives, working situations to your advantage? Or is 'ulterior motive' something that everyone is capable of, but only a select few actually utilise? An array of questions and hypotheticals again that I can't give a definitive answer to. Take a moment to reflect on your own thoughts about the matter.

Cognitive bias and leadership

Cognitive biases are 'systematic errors in thinking, that can automatically occur' (Van Mulukom, 2018). Cognitive biases occur because we view the world through the lens of our own experiences, memories and situations we have been in. Our objective understanding of any given situation is actually very limited. When considering a given situation, we place that limited objective understanding into our intuition and that's what informs our judgement. I was actually quite disappointed to learn about cognitive bias as I honestly thought my intuition was the most bullet-proof way to judge a situation and make a decision.

If we take on this idea – that we don't always have the 'understanding' we need to judge or reason with a situation, even when it has been encountered before – then really our cognitive bias does overrule our intuition, subconsciously. This research has informed my judgement and has altered my perception about intuition.

Until recently, I thought my intuition was serving as a strong and qualified source of information, but after reading up on cognitive bias I am now convinced otherwise and can see why using our intuition as the deciding factor in a situation may not always be effective, especially when you are in a position of leadership. 'Because intuition relies on evolutionarily older, automatic and fast processing, it also falls prey to misguidances, such as cognitive biases.' (Van Mulukom, 2018)

I think it's important to remember that you will already have formed judgements and opinions that come into play, even when intuition is involved. So be reflective and be aware of these pre-conceived judgements when you make decisions. That's why it's best not to make 'knee jerk' decisions but instead to take your time and think them through. If someone asks you to make a decision, say, 'Can I get back to you?' in the first instance. This will give you time to reflect, monitor your response and check in with how you really feel. In a position of responsibility, which we all have – we are responsible for our class, our TAs or LSAs, our team or our school – we absolutely need to ensure that we give the most informed response we're capable of giving. It may not be the response that colleagues want, but by pausing to consider our cognitive biases before giving a response, we are treating them humanely and with respect.

Thought capsule
Always try to be upfront and forthright in what you say and do. It's better to be politely honest than resigning yourself to swallowing important thoughts and feelings. It also benefits others around you when they know they are receiving honest, humane and genuine treatment.

Conclusion

After reflecting upon my experiences over the last 11 or so years, I wanted to try to reach out to those other educators who may have gone through, or are indeed still going through, similar scenarios. It was a case of 'what can I do to help?'.

I am incredibly grateful for contributions to my book and I know these contributions have enriched the content considerably. So thank you to those who took the time to reflect upon their positive and negative experiences and share those with me.

One last point I would like to make: if you are not being treated as you should, you can shift. Believe in yourself and your abilities; you are not a tree and who knows – where you move on to may be perfect for you: trust, autonomy, a leadership team who self-reflect and everything else in between.

Trust your instincts and remember that it's your career – own it. Your choices will make the difference to how you feel.

Thank you for reading and I hope these experiences and reflections have allowed you to consider what being an emotionally intelligent teacher and leader is all about.

Niomi Clyde Roberts

References

Angelou, M. (2009). *I Know Why the Caged Bird Sings*. New York: Random House.

Berry, J. (2016) *Making the Leap: Moving from Deputy to Head*. Carmarthen: Crown House Publishing.

Berry, J. (2019) *Emotional Intelligence and Teaching/Leading* [email].

Bono, J. and Ilies, R. (2006) Charisma, positive emotions and mood contagion. *The Leadership Quarterly*. 17(4), 317–334.

Brown, B. (2013) *Brené Brown on Empathy* [online]. Available at: https://www.ted.com/talks/brene_brown_the_power_of_vulnerability/transcript?language=en [accessed 12.11.19].

Cambridge Advanced Learner's Dictionary & Thesaurus, (2013) https://dictionary.cambridge.org/dictionary/english/ulterior

Cooper, F. (2020) [Twitter] 26 July. Available at: https://twitter.com/FloraSCooper/status/1287475644067188738 [accessed 18.11.21].

Cowley, A. (2019) *The Wellbeing Toolkit: Sustaining, Supporting and Enabling School Staff*. London: Bloomsbury.

Curran, A. (2021) https://www.independentthinking.co.uk/associates/dr-andrew-curran

Education Endowment Foundation (2021) 'Working with Parents to Support Children's Learning', https://educationendowmentfoundation.org.uk/education-evidence/guidance-reports/supporting-parents

Goldsmith, M. and Reiter, M. (2015) *Triggers: Sparking positive change and making it last*. London: Profile Books.

Goleman, D. (1995) *Emotional Intelligence: Why it Can Matter More than IQ*. London: Bloomsbury.

Goleman, D. (1998) *Working with Emotional Intelligence*. London: Bloomsbury.

Goleman, D. (2000a), 'An EI-based theory of performance' in C. Cherniss and D. Goleman (eds), *The Emotionally Intelligent Workplace: How to Select for, Measure, and Improve Emotional Intelligence in Individuals, Groups, and Organizations*. San Francisco, CA: Jossey-Bass.

Goleman, D. (2000b), 'Emotional Intelligence: Leadership That Gets Results', *Harvard Business Review*, https://hbr.org/2000/03/leadership-that-gets-results

Goleman, D. (2013) *Focus: The Hidden Driver of Excellence*. London: Bloomsbury.

Hamilton, D. R. (2012) *The 3 Paths of Intuition* [online]. Available at: http://drdavidhamilton.com/the-3-paths-of-intuition [accessed 30.10.20].

Harris, D. (2013) *Brave Heads: How to Lead a School Without Selling your Soul*. Carmarthen: Independent Thinking Press.

Hilton, J. (2018) *Ten Traits of Resilience: Achieving Positivity and Purpose in School Leadership*. London: Bloomsbury.

Kerr, J. (2013) *Legacy: What the All Blacks Can Teach Us About the Business of Life*. London: Constable.

Kolb, A. Y and Kolb, D. A. (2017) *The Experiential Educator: Principles and Practices of Experiential Learning*. USA: EBLS Press.

Lear, J. (2019) *The Monkey-Proof Box: Curriculum Design for Building Knowledge, Developing Creative Thinking and Promoting Independence*. Carmarthen: Independent Thinking Press.

Mulder, P. (2015) *McClelland Motivation Theory* [online]. Available at: www.toolshero.com/psychology/mcclelland-theory-of-motivation [accessed 30.10.20].

Mullin, S. (2019) *What They Didn't Teach Me on my PGCE: And Other Routes Into Teaching*. Canada: Word & Deed Publishing.

Myatt, M. (2016) *High Challenge Low Threat*. Woodbridge: John Catt Educational Limited.

Norman, D. (2005) *Emotional Design: Why We Love (or Hate) Everyday Things.*
New York: Perseus Books.

Pandemic: How to Prevent an Outbreak. An American documentary, shown on Netflix, January 22nd, 2020.

Pink, H. D. (2009) *Drive: The Surprising Truth about What Motivates Us.* USA: Riverhead Books.

Steiner, I. D. (1972). *Group Processes and Productivity.* USA: Academic Press.

Strickland, S. (2020) *Education Exposed: Leading a School in a Time of Uncertainty.* Woodbridge: John Catt.

Tierney, J. and Baumeister, R. F. (2019) *The Power of Bad: And How to Overcome It.* UK, USA: Penguin.

Tierney, J. and Baumeister, R. F. (2020) *Life is mostly good, despite the greater power of bad things* [online]. Available at: https://thepsychologist.bps.org.uk/volume-33/march-2020/life-mostly-good-despite-greater-power-bad-things [accessed 17.11.21].

Van Mulukom, V. (2018) *Is it Rational to Trust Your Gut Instincts? A Neuroscientist Explains* [online]. Available at: https://theconversation.com/is-it-rational-to-trust-your-gut-feelings-a-neuroscientist-explains-95086 [accessed 22.08.19].

Zetlin, M. (2021) *In 9 Words, Serena Williams Just Taught a Major Lesson in Emotional Intelligence* [online]. Available at: www.inc.com/minda-zetlin/serena-williams-australian-open-press-conference-crying-tears-loss-naomi-osaka.html [accessed 22.02.21].

Index